ABOUT THE AUTHOR

Anthony Robbins has devoted more than half his life to helping people discover and develop their own unique qualities of greatness. Considered the nation's leader in the science of peak performance, he is the founder and chairman of the Anthony Robbins Companies, which are committed to assisting people in achieving personal and professional mastery. Mr Robbins lives in California with his wife and children.

'Anthony Robbins has reached us on yet another level by offering *Giant Steps*. Here is another chance for us to reach out to fellow human beings who are seeking greater depth in their lives by embracing our personal vision throughout the year'

Dr Deepak Chopra

'With *Giant Steps*, I can now access Anthony Robbins' technology every day, feeling as if I have a ready-made coach at hand supporting and prompting me to stretch for the highest levels of creativity, leadership and humanitarianism'

Ken Blanchard, author of the *One-Minute Manager* series

'Tony thinks differently, and thank god he does, because he helps us to think differently about everything. Talk about value added leadership!'
Mike Basch, Federal Express

'Robbins is a great public speaker, the best I have ever heard'
Martyn Harris, *Daily Telegraph*

GIANT STEPS

Small Changes to Make a Big Difference:
Daily Lessons in Self-Mastery

ANTHONY ROBBINS

POCKET BOOKS
New York London Toronto Sydney Singapore

First published in Great Britain by Simon & Schuster UK Ltd, 1994
This edition first published by Pocket Books, 2001
An imprint of Simon & Schuster Ltd
A CBS COMPANY

Copyright © Anthony Robbins, 1994

16

Simon & Schuster UK Ltd
1st Floor, 222 Gray's Inn Road,
London
WC1X 8HB

www.simonandschuster.co.uk

Simon & Schuster Australia, Sydney

A CIP catalogue record for this book is available from the British Library

ISBN 13: 978-0-7434-0936-0

Printed and bound by CPI Group (UK) Ltd, Croydon, CR0 4YY

GIANT
STEPS

CONTENTS

GIANT STEPS

DREAMS OF DESTINY

DECISIONS AND GOAL SETTING

•

"Nothing happens unless first a dream."

—CARL SANDBURG

1

We all have dreams. . . . We all want to believe deep down in our souls that we have a special gift, that we can make a difference, that we can touch others in a special way, and that we can make the world a better place.

What's one of your aspirations? Maybe it's a dream you've forgotten or have begun to relinquish. If that vision were alive today, what would your life be like?

Take a moment now just to dream and to think about what you really want for your life.

2

It's not what we do once in a while that counts, but our consistent actions. And what is the father of all action? What ultimately determines who we become and where we go in life? The answer is our *decisions*. It's in these moments that our destiny is shaped. More than anything else, I believe **our decisions—not the conditions of our lives— determine our destiny.**

3

Who would have thought that the conviction of a quiet, unassuming man—a lawyer by trade and a pacifist by principle—would have the power to topple a vast empire? Yet Mahatma Gandhi's decision, his belief in nonviolence as a means to helping India's people regain control of their country, set in motion an unexpected chain of events.

Realize the power of a single decision acted upon immediately and with utter conviction. The secret is to make a public commitment, one so forceful you cannot turn back from it. While many thought that his was an impossible dream, Gandhi's consistent commitment to his decision made it an undeniable reality.

What could you, too, accomplish if you invoked a similar level of passion, conviction, and action to create unstoppable momentum?

4

Each of us is endowed with innate resources that enable us to achieve all we've ever dreamed of—and more. **The floodgates can be opened by one decision, bringing us joy or sorrow, prosperity or poverty, companionship or solitude, long life or early death.**

I challenge you to make a decision today that can immediately change or improve the quality of your life. Do something you've been putting off ... master a new set of skills ... treat people with newfound respect and compassion ... call someone you haven't spoken to in years. Just know that *all* decisions have consequences. Even making no decision at all is a decision in its own way.

What decisions have you made or failed to make in the past that powerfully influence your life today?

5

In 1955, Rosa Parks made a decision to defy an unjust law that discriminated against her on the basis of her race. Her refusal to give up her seat on the bus had consequences far beyond those she may have been aware of at the moment. Had she intended to change the structure of a society? **No matter what her intent, her commitment to a higher standard compelled her to act.**

What far-reaching effects could be set in motion by raising the standards you hold for your life and making a true decision to live up to them today?

6

We've all heard about people who've exploded beyond the limitations of their conditions to become examples of the unlimited power of the human spirit.

You and I can make our lives one of these legendary inspirations, as well, simply by having courage and the awareness that we can control whatever happens in our lives. Although we cannot always control the events in our lives, we can always control our *response* to them, and the actions we take as a result.

If there's anything you're not happy about—in your relationships, in your health, in your career—*make a decision right now about how you're going to change it immediately.*

7

The more decisions you make, the better you'll become at making them. Muscles get stronger with use, and so it is with your decision-making muscles.

Today, make two decisions you've been putting off: one easy decision and one that's a bit more far-reaching. Immediately take the first action toward fulfilling each of them—and follow through with the next step tomorrow. By doing this, you'll be building the muscle that can change your entire life.

8

We must commit to learning from our mistakes instead of agonizing over them, or we're destined to repeat our errors in the future. When you temporarily run aground, remember that there are no failures in life. There are only results. Consider the adage: **Success is the result of good judgment, good judgment is the result of experience, and experience is often the result of bad judgment!**

What have you learned from a past mistake that you can use to improve your life today?

9

Success and failure **are usually not the result of a single event.** Failure is the result of neglecting to make the call...to go the extra mile ...to say, "I love you." In the same way that failure follows this string of small decisions, success comes from taking the initiative and following up...persisting...eloquently expressing the depth of your love.

What simple action could you take today to produce a new momentum toward success in your life?

10

Research has consistently shown that **those who succeed tend to make decisions rapidly** and are slow to reverse a well-thought-out position. Conversely, people who fail usually decide slowly and change their minds frequently. Once you've made a sound decision, stick by it!

11

He's spent nearly half his life in an iron lung and the other half in a wheelchair. With so many personal challenges, surely he's been in no position to improve the quality of life for others. Or has he?

Ed Roberts personifies the power of a single, committed moment of decision. He became the first quadriplegic to graduate from the University of California, Berkeley, and served as director of the California State Department of Rehabilitation. A tireless advocate for disabled people, he has lobbied to secure all persons' right of access and supplied many of the innovations that made these laws enforceable.

There are no excuses. *Make three decisions now that will change your health, your career, your relationships, your life—and act upon them.*

12

How do you turn the invisible into the visible? The first step is to define your dream precisely; **the only limit to what you can achieve is the extent of your ability to define with precision that which you desire.** Let's begin now to crystallize your dreams, and over the next few days form a plan that will ensure their attainment.

13

We all have goals, whether we know it or not. No matter what they are, they have a profound effect on our lives. Yet some of our goals, such as "I need to pay my lousy bills," lack any inspiration. **The secret of unleashing your true power is setting goals that are exciting enough that they truly inspire your creativity and ignite your passion.**

Right now, consciously choose your goals. Brainstorm everything worth pursuing. Then pick a goal that excites you the most, something that will get you up early and keep you up late. Assign a deadline for achieving it, and write a paragraph describing why you absolutely must attain it by then. Is it grand enough to challenge you? to push you beyond your limits? to uncover your true potential?

14

Have you ever bought a new outfit or car, then started spotting it everywhere? Surely it's always been around you. Why haven't you noticed it until now?

Quite simply, a portion of your brain is responsible for screening out all information except what's essential to your survival and success. **So much that could help you achieve your dreams is never noticed or utilized simply because you haven't defined (taught your brain what's important!) your goals with clarity.**

Once you do, however, you'll have triggered your Reticular Activating System (RAS). This part of your mind becomes like a magnet, attracting any information or opportunities that can help you achieve your goals more rapidly. Tripping this powerful neurological switch can literally transform your life in a matter of days or weeks.

15

GUIDELINES FOR GOAL SETTING (Programming Your RAS)

1) Commit now to spending ten minutes each day for the next four days setting goals. (*NOTE:* Keep a permanent record of these goals in a hardbound journal.)

2) As you work on the goal-setting exercises, constantly ask yourself, "What would I want for my life if I knew I could have it any way I wanted it? What would I do if I knew I could not fail?"

3) Have fun! Imagine that you are a kid again. You're in a department store on Christmas Eve, about to sit on Santa's lap. (Remember what this was like?) In this state of excited anticipation, nothing is too big to ask for, nothing costs too much, everything is within reach...

16

DAY #1: PERSONAL DEVELOPMENT GOALS

Your sense of personal well-being and enrichment lays the foundation for every other achievement in your life.

1) Take five minutes to brainstorm all the possibilities: *What would you like to learn? What skills do you want to master? What character traits would you like to develop? Who would your friends be? Who would you be?*

2) Give each of your goals a timeline (6 months, 1 year, 5 years, 10 years, 20 years) for completion.

3) Highlight your top one-year goal.

4) In two minutes, write a brief paragraph stating why you are absolutely committed to achieving this goal within the next year.

17

DAY #2: CAREER/BUSINESS/ECONOMIC GOALS

Whether you aspire **to being at the top of your profession amassing millions or a professional student gaining a wealth of knowledge, now is your chance to be sure it counts.**

1) Take five minutes to brainstorm all the possibilities: *How much money do you want to accumulate? What do you wish to achieve with your career/company? How much do you wish to earn annually? What financial decisions do you need to make?*
2) Give each of your goals a timeline (6 months, 1 year, 5 years, 10 years, 20 years) for completion.
3) Highlight your top one-year goal.
4) In two minutes, write a brief paragraph stating why you are absolutely committed to achieving this goal within the next year.

18

DAY #3: TOYS/ADVENTURE GOALS

If you had no financial limitations, **what are some of the things you'd like to have or experience? If a genie were before you now, waiting to obey your every command, what would you wish for?**

1) Take five minutes to brainstorm all the possibilities: *What would you like to build or purchase? What events would you like to attend? What adventures would you like to experience?*

2) Give each of your goals a timeline (6 months, 1 year, 5 years, 10 years, 20 years) for completion.

3) Highlight your top one-year goal.

4) In two minutes, write a brief paragraph stating why you are absolutely committed to achieving this goal within the next year.

19

DAY #4: CONTRIBUTION GOALS

This is your opportunity **to leave your mark, to create a legacy that makes a true difference in people's lives.**

1) Take five minutes to brainstorm all the possibilities: *How can you contribute? Who or what can you help? What can you create?*
2) Give each of your goals a timeline (6 months, 1 year, 5 years, 10 years, 20 years) for completion.
3) Highlight your top one-year goal.
4) In two minutes, write a brief paragraph stating why you are absolutely committed to achieving this goal within the next year.

20

Never leave the site of a goal without first taking some form of positive action toward its attainment. Right now, take a moment to define the first steps you must take to achieve your goal. **What can you do today to move yourself forward?** Even the smallest step—a phone call, a commitment, sketching out an initial plan—will put you closer to your goal. Then develop a list of simple things you can do every day for the next ten days. These ten days of creating a chain of habits and building unstoppable momentum will ensure your long-term success. *Begin now!*

21

How would you feel if you had mastered and attained all your goals a year from now? How would you feel about yourself? How would you feel about your life? Answering these questions will help you develop compelling reasons to achieve your goals. **Having a powerful enough *why* will provide you with the necessary *how*.**

Take this opportunity to brainstorm your top four one-year goals. Under each one, write a paragraph about why you are absolutely committed to achieving these goals within the year.

22

The secret to achieving your goals is mental conditioning. Review them at least twice daily. *Post your goals where you're sure to see them every day:* in your journal, on your desk, in your wallet, or over your bathroom mirror so you can look at them while you're shaving or putting on makeup. **Remember, whatever you consistently think about and focus upon, you move toward.** This is a simple yet important way to program your RAS for success.

23

If your first attempt at achieving your goals seems futile, should you move on and do something else? Absolutely not!

Persistence overshadows even talent as the most valuable resource in shaping the quality of life. After all, no one ever achieved a goal by being *interested* in its achievement; one must be *committed.* **Isn't it possible that short-term "failures" may actually provide you with the necessary insights or distinctions to create even greater success in the future?** Of course!

As you look back now over your "unsuccessful" attempts in the past, what have you learned? How can you use these insights to create great success, now and in the future?

24

All people who succeed consciously or unconsciously utilize the same formula for success. *Use these four simple steps to achieve whatever you desire.*

THE ULTIMATE SUCCESS FORMULA

1) Decide what you want. (Be precise! Clarity is power.)

2) Take action (because desire is not enough).

3) Notice what's working or not. (You don't want to continue to expend energy on an approach that's worthless.)

4) Change your approach until you achieve what you want. (Flexibility gives you the power to create a new approach and a new result.)

25

In pursuit of our goals, we often set in motion far-reaching consequences. Does the honeybee deliberate on how to propagate flowers? No, but in the process of seeking sweet nectar, the bee unknowingly gathers pollen on its legs, flies to the next flower, and sets in motion a wondrous chain reaction that results in a hillside awash in color.

In the same way, your pursuit of worthwhile goals has probably resulted in unforeseen benefits for others. Maybe it was the simple decision to call an old friend once a month, which has resulted in all sorts of pluses you didn't even anticipate.

In how many ways will other people benefit from your efforts today?

26

The real purpose of a goal is what it makes of you as a human being while you pursue it. **Who you become as a person is the ultimate reward.**

Take a moment now to write a brief paragraph describing all the character traits, skills, abilities, attitudes, and beliefs you need to develop to achieve all of your goals.

27

Don't put off joy and happiness. To so many people, goal setting means that only someday, after they've achieved something great, will they be able to enjoy life. **There's a huge difference between achieving to be happy and happily achieving.** Strive to live each day to its fullest, squeezing all the joy you can out of each moment. Instead of measuring your life's value by your progress toward a single goal, remember that the direction you're headed in is more important than temporary results.

What is your current direction? Are you moving toward your goals or away from them? Do you need to make a course correction? Are you enjoying life to the fullest? *If not, make a change in one of these areas now.*

28

How many times have you heard the lament "Is that all there is?"

The Apollo astronauts, who had prepared nearly their entire lives for their moon landing, were euphoric in their historic moment of glory, yet upon returning to earth some became terribly depressed. After all, what was left to look forward to? What could be a bigger goal than making it to the moon, exploring outer space? Perhaps the answer is to be found in exploring an equally uncharted frontier: the *inner space* of the mind and heart.

We all need a continued sense of emotional and spiritual growth; it is the food on which our souls thrive. As you approach the attainment of the goals you've pursued, be sure to immediately design for yourself a new, compelling future.

29

What is the ultimate goal? Perhaps it is aspiring to contribute something of value. **Finding a way to help others—those we care about deeply—can inspire us for a lifetime.** There is always a place in the world for those who are willing to give of their time, energy, capital, creativity, and commitment.

What simple act of kindness could you show another person today? Decide now, take action, and be sure to appreciate how this makes you feel.

30

Venerable comedian George Burns understands the importance of having something to look forward to. Summing up his life philosophy he said, "You have to have something to get you out of bed. I can't do anything in bed, anyway. **The most important thing is to have a point, a direction you're headed."** Now in his nineties, he's still sharpening his wit, still taking on movie and TV projects, and booked himself for a performance at the London Palladium in the year 2000—when he'll be 104 years old! How's that for creating a compelling future?

Most people overestimate what they can do in a year and underestimate what they can do in a decade. *What will* you *be doing ten years from now?*

31

Think of something you enjoy or experience today that once was merely a goal. Many obstacles may have intervened in your pursuit of its attainment, yet now it's part of your life. As you follow your new dreams and encounter obstacles, remember: you've been through this before, and you've succeeded!

The human spirit is truly unconquerable. The will to win—the will to succeed, to shape one's life, to take control—can be harnessed only when you decide what you want and believe that no challenge, no problem, no obstacle can keep you from it. Obstacles are merely a call to strengthen your resolve to achieve your worthwhile goals.

HOW TO GET WHAT YOU REALLY WANT

PAIN/PLEASURE AND MENTAL STATE

●

"Every great and commanding moment in the annals of the world is the triumph of some enthusiasm."

—RALPH WALDO EMERSON

32

To get what you want, you must discover what's preventing you from taking action. Think of something you avoided doing until the last minute: your taxes, for example. Isn't it true that you put it off simply to avoid the pain of the moment, only to experience even greater pain later on?

But what happens on April 14? Our procrastination disappears because we quickly change what we believe (associate in our minds) will bring us pain or pleasure. Suddenly, *not* taking action is much more painful than just doing it.

How can you use this to change your life? In the future, instead of asking, "How can I avoid doing this painful task?" ask, "If I don't take action now, what will this ultimately cost me?"

Pain can be your friend if you use it effectively.

33

Are we merely animals responding like Pavlov's dog to punishment and reward? Of course not. **One of the miracles of being human is that we can *decide* what causes us pain and pleasure.** A hunger striker, for example, can undergo physical pain yet transform the experience into moral pleasure by focusing on the positive impact of calling the world's attention to a worthwhile cause.

Each of us has this power of choice. The secret of success is learning how to use pain and pleasure to your advantage.

Is there an area of your life in which you feel unnecessary pain? Are you perhaps reacting rather than deliberately choosing? How could you change your focus and turn a seemingly painful event into a pleasurable opportunity to learn, grow, or help others?

34

What you link pain to **and what you link pleasure to shape your destiny.** Each of us has learned and adopted a unique pattern of behaviors to get ourselves out of pain and into pleasure. Some people do this by drinking, smoking, overeating, or verbally abusing others. Others do it by exercising, conversing, learning, helping others, or making a difference in some way.

What are some of your pain-avoiding and pleasure-inducing patterns? How have they shaped your life up until now? Make a list of these strategies. When you want to feel better, do you watch TV? light a cigarette? go to sleep? What are some of the more positive ways in which you could move away from pain and toward pleasure?

35

For most people, their fear of loss is much greater than their desire for gain. **Most individuals would work much harder to hang on to what they have than to take the necessary risks to shoot for their dreams.**

Which would drive you more: keeping someone from stealing $100,000 you'd earned over the last five years, or acting on an opportunity to earn $100,000 in the next five years?

36

Often when we see greatness in others we assume they are just more fortunate, blessed with special gifts. **In reality they have utilized a greater depth of their human resources simply because failing to be, do, and share their all would be the ultimate pain for them.** The selfless life of Mother Teresa, for example, is driven by the clear relationship she has made between anyone else's pain and her own. This drives her to help *anyone* who suffers anywhere in the world. Her ultimate pleasure is alleviating their pain. (But, as we'll explore later, this was not always true.)

What gives you the most pain and the most pleasure, and how does this shape your life today?

37

Mixed emotions are behind most patterns of self-sabotage, and they certainly limit the level of enjoyment and success one can experience in life.

For example, people often say they'd like to earn more money. Certainly they have the ingenuity and intelligence to figure out how to accomplish this. What stops them is mixed emotions or *mixed associations.* They may believe that amassing wealth would give them more freedom, security, and ability to help those they love. Simultaneously, they may associate having "excess" money to being wasteful, shallow, and manipulative.

If you've ever found yourself taking two steps forward and one step back, invariably it's because you have mixed associations; i.e., you associate achieving your goal to both pain and pleasure.

Do you have mixed associations that affect your life?

38

Is there an area of your life you'd like to measurably improve—such as your finances or relationships—but something seems to be holding you back?

Write your answer on a piece of paper and draw a line down the center of the page. On the left, list all the negative emotions you have about it, and on the right the positive.

Are there more minuses than pluses? Is there one negative association that outweighs all the positive associations combined? Does the (im)balance reflect the results you've produced until today?

Under the bright light of conscious scrutiny negative associations often lose their hold on you; awareness is the first step.

39

Have you ever felt that no matter what you do you'll get pain? For example, sometimes people feel that if they stay in a relationship they'll be miserable, but if they leave they'll be alone—and even more miserable. As a result, they do nothing... and feel miserable!

Rather than feeling trapped, use your pain as your strongest ally. Think about what you've experienced in the past and the present. Feel the pain with such emotional intensity that it gives you the leverage to finally do something about it. We call this reaching *emotional threshold*. Instead of passively waiting for this inevitable emotion, why not consciously and actively produce it in a way that motivates you to make your life better, starting today?

40

Willpower never works—at least not long term. Have you ever had the experience of hitting emotional threshold, let's say with your body, where you've "had it!"? What did you do? Maybe you denied yourself, employing the willpower strategy of dieting. But, of course, any result you got was short lived because denying yourself food is always painful, and your brain will not allow you to continuously experience pain when there is an alternative.

So what's the solution? **Instead of fighting your natural instincts, simply change what you associate** to food until you've conditioned pain to this pattern. Consistently remember the negative feelings you've experienced after overindulging. Make overeating painful and exercising pleasurable—and you will be irresistibly drawn to do the right things.

41

One of my definitions of success is to live your life in a way that causes you to consistently feel an immense amount of pleasure and very little pain—and because of your lifestyle, to have the people around you consistently feel a lot more pleasure and very little pain. To do this, **we must grow and contribute.**

How successful are you, by this definition? What could you do today to enjoy yourself more, or to give even more to those around you?

42

Procrastination is one of the most common ways to avoid pain. **But usually if you delay taking action, you only create more pain for yourself later on.**

What are four actions you've been putting off that need your attention today? Make a list, then answer the following questions:

1) Why haven't I taken this action? In the past, what pain have I linked to doing it?

2) What pleasure have I had in the past by indulging in this negative pattern?

3) What will it cost me if I don't change now? How does that make me feel?

4) What pleasure will I receive by taking each of these actions right now?

43

Have you ever done something and thought afterward, "How could I?! That was so stupid!" Conversely, have you ever done something then thought to yourself, "That was amazing! How did I pull that off? I'm impressed."

What determines the difference between acting badly or brilliantly? Rarely is it based solely on your ability. Instead, it's the *state* of your mind and/or body in any given moment that shapes the way you think, feel, behave, and perform. If you know the secret of accessing your most powerful mental/emotional states, you can literally work wonders. In the right state of mind, ideas and abilities flow in a seemingly effortless fashion.

What could you accomplish if you lived in a peak state every day?

44

We've all been sold a bill of goods. We've been taught that someday, when all the right things happen, we'll finally be happy. When we find the ideal mate... when we earn enough money... when our body is perfect... when we have children... when we finally retire.

The truth is, what you get will not make you feel good, but learning how to change your state of mind in an instant will. After all, why do you want any of these things? Isn't it because you believe the ideal mate, children, money, etc., will make you *feel better?* But when we finally have those things we're pursuing, who'll make us feel good? We do it to ourselves. Why wait? *Do it now!*

45

Do you know how to make yourself feel good? If you wanted to feel completely happy, excited, and ecstatic right now, could you? You bet! **Just change your focus.**

Remember a time when you felt absolutely on top of the world? Picture it all in vivid detail... Listen to the sounds around you... Feel your pulse race! Breathe the way you were breathing, put the same expression on your face, and move your body just as you did then. Do you feel even a hint of that excitement again? *Is it possible that you could feel this way anytime you want?*

46

There are unlimited ways of perceiving and experiencing anything in life. Any sensation is available at any moment—all you have to do is tune in to the right channel. How? **There are two secrets for changing your emotional state instantly.** The first is to shift your mental *focus*.

Think of one of the most treasured memories of your life. As you remember it now, how does it make you feel? What else could you focus on that would make you feel great?

Tomorrow we'll investigate the second way to change your emotional state instantly.

47

Changing focus is only one way to change your emotional state. A quicker, more powerful way is to use your physical body, or your *physiology*. For example, when most people don't like how they feel, they drink alcohol, eat, smoke, sleep, use drugs. Or they use positive strategies such as dancing, singing, exercising, or making love.

Every emotion you feel has a specific physiology attached to it. When people are depressed, what's their posture? Their shoulders droop, their head hangs down, their breathing becomes shallow, their facial expression is slack. Conversely, when we say we're feeling happy and "up," our shoulders rise, our head lifts, our breathing is full. We can consciously command these changes in our physiology and immediately produce the emotional states we desire.

48

Some of the simplest things **can make the biggest difference.** If you want to create a fun habit that will benefit you in unexpected ways, try the following exercise.

Commit for the next seven days to spending one minute, five times a day, in front of the mirror doing nothing but grinning from ear to ear. This may feel pretty foolish at first, but by repeating it several times a day, you'll consistently spark your nervous system to generate feelings of happiness, spontaneity, humor, and silliness. Most important, you'll condition yourself to feel good and develop the physical habit of happiness. Take a moment to do this now, and make it fun!

49

Age is more a matter of focus and physiology than chronology. Many people have lived many years but still have a "skip" in their walk and flexibility in their thought.

A simple example of this is found on a rainy day. When "old" people see a puddle, what do they do? They not only walk around it, they complain the whole time!

On the other hand, children—and those still young at heart—might jump right in, laugh, splash around, and have a good time.

Enjoy life's "puddles." Live with a spring in your step, a smile on your face. Make cheerfulness, outrageousness, and playfulness new priorities for your life. You're alive! *You can feel good for no reason at all!*

50

One of the best ways to enrich your life is to expand your emotional range. How many emotions do you consistently feel in an average week? *Make a list.*

Now review it. If you have fewer than a dozen emotions, add those you'd love to experience on a more consistent basis. Most people experience only a fraction of the thousands of emotions available to them.

Realize that you can expand your range of emotions just by directing your focus and changing your physiology. Pick one of the positive emotions you'd like to feel, and right now, stand the way you'd be standing if you were feeling this way already. Move, gesture, and speak in a tone of voice consistent with this emotion. Enjoy the immediate change in how you feel!

51

Have you ever been in a situation that drove you crazy with anger, frustration, or feeling overwhelmed—yet today, years later, you can look back and laugh at the very thing that bothered you so much? We've all heard the old adage "Someday you'll look back on this and laugh." One of my teachers, NLP co-founder Richard Bandler, once asked, Why wait? **Why not laugh at it *now*?**

Try this today. Laugh at something you previously thought was unbelievably stressful. Do you feel like you're a little more in charge of the situation?

52

Have you ever expected your spouse to be home at a certain time, yet he or she was late? Maybe you assumed that your spouse didn't care enough to be punctual. Perhaps you feared that there had been an accident on the way home. You might have imagined your spouse stopping somewhere to buy you a surprise.

Whatever we focus on determines how we feel. And how we feel —our state of mind—powerfully influences our actions and interactions. Rather than jump to conclusions, consider all the possibilities and choose to focus on one that will empower you and those you care about.

53

A fantastic analogy for the power of focus is racing cars. When your car begins to skid, the natural reflex is to look at the wall in an attempt to avoid it. **But if you keep focusing on what you fear, that's exactly where you'll end up.** Professional racers know that we unconsciously steer in the direction of our focus, so with their lives on the line, they turn their focus away from the wall and toward the open track.

In life, most people focus on what they don't want instead of what they do. If you resist your fear, have faith, and discipline your focus, your actions will naturally take you in the direction you want. *Release your fear, and focus now on what you truly desire and deserve.*

54

Emotion is created by motion. Next time you're getting ready to jog but don't feel 100 percent eager to do it, why not go out for a skip instead? Skipping is such a powerful way to change your state because:

1) It's great exercise.
2) It causes less stress on your body than running.
3) You won't be able to keep a straight face.
4) You'll entertain anyone who drives by!

55

The most effective way to control your focus is through the use of questions. **For any question you pose, your brain provides an answer.** For example, if you ask, "Why is so-and-so taking advantage of me?" you can't help but focus on how you're being bilked, whether it's actually true or not. But if you ask instead, "How can I improve this situation?" you are certain to get answers that enable you to take positive action.

56

The power of asking the right questions is shown by a boy who was beat up one day by the seventh-grade bully. Vowing revenge, he got hold of a gun and tracked down his tormentor.

But just before he fired, he wondered, What will happen to me if I pull the trigger? An image more painful than anything else came into focus as he visualized a life in jail. He re-aimed and shot a tree instead.

This boy was Bo Jackson. **One shift in focus, one decision weighing pain against pleasure, probably made the difference between a kid with no future and a kid who would become one of our greatest sports legends.**

What life-changing questions could you ask yourself today?

57

Has anyone ever told you, "You have a bright future"? How did that make you feel? What if somebody were to say that your future is dark? Or that your plan "sounds great" versus it "cries out for improvement"? Or that your new roommate "gives me the creeps" or is "really cool"?

The difference is not just in the words, but in the feelings they produce. People who speak in terms of a bright or dark future are operating in a *visual* mode, being affected most by what they see. Other people are influenced more by what they hear ("sounds" and "cries" are *auditory*); and others' feelings are most crucial in how they perceive things ("creeps" and "cool" are *kinesthetic*).

Which of these modes most often applies to your focus?

58

What are some healthful ways to boost your emotional state without resorting to cigarettes, alcohol, food binges, credit card abuse, or anything else with negative consequences?

Let's take several minutes now to brainstorm!

1) List all the positive methods you currently use to replace painful feelings with pleasurable ones instantly.

2) Add some new ways you may never have tried before but which you think could positively change your state as well. Don't stop until you have at least 15 ideas written down, preferably 25 or more. This is an exercise you'll probably want to repeat until you've discovered *hundreds* of healthy ways to change your state!

59

To travel the "high road" from pain to pleasure, **discover numerous positive ways to change your outlook.** Consider some of these strategies:

Sing along with your favorite music . . . read something that offers information you can immediately apply . . . laugh at a funny movie or show . . . swim several laps . . . share a meal with your family or with a friend . . . dance . . . soak in a warm tub . . . come up with five new ideas . . . get to know a stranger . . . tell silly jokes to friends, knowing they'll probably still like you anyway . . . write in your journal . . . hug and kiss your spouse.

Pick one of these and try it now!

THE POWER TO CREATE, THE POWER TO DESTROY

BELIEFS

●

*"It is the mind that maketh good of ill,
that maketh wretch or happy, rich or poor."*

—EDMUND SPENSER

60

What is the force that determines what we try or fail to try to accomplish in our lives? It is our beliefs—about what we're capable of, about what's possible or impossible, about who we are. In Haitian culture, a person's belief in the deadly power of the witch doctor "pointing the bone" can indeed cause death. But the real killer is a sense of certainty—the belief—not the witch doctor.

In your own life, have you set negative expectations? What effects has this had on your life? What are some of the most empowering beliefs that have positively shaped your life? What new, positive expectations can you set for yourself and others?

61

For thousands of years it was known that no human could run a four-minute mile; it was physically impossible. Yet Roger Bannister shattered this belief when he ran a 3:59 mile. How did he do it? In his mind's eye, he repeatedly visualized his triumph so intensely that **his certainty gave an unquestioned command to his nervous system, and he achieved physical results to match his mental picture.** Following in Bannister's stride and believing that they, too, could do it, within one year several others duplicated his feat.

What barrier do you need to burst through? What do you perceive as impossible today that if you were certain it was possible—and you did it—would change not only your life but the lives of those around you?

62

So often people blame events for how their lives have turned out. **Yet what really shapes our lives is the *meaning* we attach to events.**

Two men are shot down in Vietnam, held captive, and tortured repeatedly. One man commits suicide. The other forges a deeper belief in himself, humanity, and his Creator than he ever had before. Today this man, Captain Gerald Coffee, shares his story to remind us of the power of the human spirit to overcome any level of pain, any obstacle, any problem.

Do you or does someone you know allow a past circumstance to limit today's happiness? What else could these events mean? Have they made you stronger? wiser? able to counsel others who may face the same challenges?

63

Why do people do what they do? It's all a matter of their beliefs. As amazing as it sounds, if people believe that drilling holes in their heads will cure sickness, they'll do it (and have!)—whether that belief is well-founded or not—and if they believe instead that their happiness depends on helping others, they'll be equally driven.

Beliefs make the difference between a lifetime of misery and one of joyous contribution. **Beliefs separate a Mozart from a Manson, causing some individuals to become heroes while others resign themselves to wondering what could have been.**

What beliefs are at work in the actions of those around you? Which beliefs do you share with your colleagues? your children? your parents? Which differ?

64

Whenever anything happens to you, your brain asks two questions: Will this mean pain or pleasure? What must I do now to avoid pain and/or gain pleasure? The answers are based on *generalizations—the beliefs you've formed about what leads to pain and pleasure.* While such shortcuts allow us to function, they can also severely limit our lives. Some people, for example, have generalized that they're incompetent because they've occasionally failed to follow up, and unfortunately, generalizations can become self-fulfilling prophecies.

Think of a limiting characterization you may have made about yourself or someone else. Do you really have sound reasons for it? What exceptions are there? Is it possible that your generalization is *too* general?

65

Nothing in life has any meaning except the meaning we give it. **One of the marvels of being human is our ability to fill any event with uplifting or devastating significance.**

Some people have taken the pain of the past and decided, "Because of this I'll never love again or be complete." Still others have shown the transformation that a more empowering meaning can create: "Because I was treated unfairly, I will be more sensitive to others' needs," or "Because I lost my child, I will work to make the world a safer place."

No matter what happens, we *all* have the capacity to create meanings that empower us. *Revolutionize your life by creating a new meaning for a past experience.*

66

Beliefs have the power to create **and the power to destroy.** Because of their amazing influence on our lives, we must understand these three challenges:

1) Most of us do not consciously decide what we're going to believe.
2) Often our beliefs are based on a misinterpretation of the past.
3) Once we adopt a belief, we tend to consider it gospel and forget that it's only one perspective.

Do you have any beliefs you take for granted to be true? What are some contrary beliefs that might also be true? How would your life be different if you adopted the opposite view?

67

A belief is nothing more than a feeling of certainty about what something means. For example, if you believe you're intelligent, then it's more than just an idea; you *feel certain* you are intelligent. Where did that sense of certainty come from?

Imagine an idea as a tabletop. Without legs, nothing supports it. To become a belief, an idea-tabletop must have legs. These legs of certainty are provided through *reference experiences*. If you believe you're intelligent, for example, you've probably had experiences (references) of doing well in school, being told you're smart, etc.

However, **we're not limited to our past as a source of certainty.** Like Roger Bannister, we can use our imagination to create references for—and certainty about—things we've yet to even attempt.

68

We can turn any idea into a belief if we just provide enough reference experiences to support it. Which one of these statements is true?

1) People are basically honest and decent.
2) People are dishonest and look out only for themselves.

If you wanted to, don't you have enough experiences (references) to back up the belief that people are basically rotten? If you focused on other experiences, couldn't you just as easily find evidence that people are basically honest?

Which one of these beliefs is really true? **Whichever belief you construct is the one that will be true for you.**

69

While an unshakable sense of certainty can help you accomplish great things, it also has the potential to blind you to the very information that could change your life forever.

Have you ever met someone who, out of a need to stay certain, wouldn't listen to new ideas?

If you were to take a look at your own beliefs through someone else's eyes, what would you see?

70

Beliefs drive all of our behavior. While some affect only one aspect of our lives, others are more pervasive. For example, a specific belief like "John is dishonest" would influence your interactions with John, but believing *"People* are dishonest" would have ramifications far beyond one relationship.

Global beliefs like this one are usually based on some generalization made long ago under extreme circumstances. We may have completely forgotten it, yet *unconsciously* we still allow it to guide our decision making.

The effect these beliefs can have on our lives is unlimited, but this does not have to be negative: Change one global belief and you change every aspect of your life for the better.

71

Are some beliefs more powerful than others? Absolutely. **There are three different levels of certainty: *opinion, belief,* and *conviction.*** **Opinions** can be shifted easily, as they are based on transitory perceptions. **Beliefs** are much stronger because they're based either on many experiences or on experiences with more emotion attached to them. It's still possible to destabilize this certainty with new questions. A **conviction,** on the other hand, is buttressed by such high emotional intensity that the person holding it not only feels certain, but can actually become enraged and/or blinded to any rational discussion if the conviction is even questioned.

Convictions can be incredibly empowering or unbelievably destructive. *Which of your beliefs are opinions?* Which do you feel more strongly about? Do any of them approach the level of conviction?

72

What's the purpose of a belief? It guides us in making decisions about how to avoid pain or gain pleasure more quickly. Because of our beliefs, we don't have to continually start from scratch in making those decisions. **Sometimes in our moments of greatest fear, pain, or emotional intensity, we look for relief in the form of a belief.** Do you know, for example, anyone who has turned pain over a hurtful relationship into a conviction that he or she will never find love?

Some people with convictions will resist all information to the contrary; at their most extreme, they'd rather suffer excruciating pain— loneliness, depression, even death—than give up their beliefs.

Do you have convictions? Which ones empower or disempower you?

91

73

Because of the passion they inspire in us, **convictions propel us to action.** Someone who cares deeply about the rights of animals has a belief, but someone who spends spare time passionately educating the public about such issues as laboratory testing and the consequences of eating a meat-based diet has a conviction.

Are there areas of your life in which holding a conviction would give you the added drive to push through all kinds of obstacles? For example, can you see how the conviction never to let yourself become overweight would compel you to make healthy lifestyle choices consistently? Do you realize how a conviction like "I can always find a way to turn things around" could help steer you through the toughest times?

74

Think of the far-reaching effects on your life if you only had a stronger sense of certainty to **back up your empowering beliefs.**
   Use the following exercise to boost your level of commitment.

1) Select a belief you wish to raise to the level of a conviction.
2) Add new and stronger references to this belief. For example, if you've decided never to eat meat again, talk to people who lead vegetarian or vegan lifestyles to discover how this choice has affected them.
3) Find or create a triggering event that produces strong emotional intensity. For example, if you've vowed to give up smoking, visit the intensive-care wing of a hospital to observe emphysema patients.
4) Whether your steps are big or small, start acting on your conviction.

75

The power of beliefs is dramatically demonstrated by case studies of people with multiple personality disorder. **Because of the strength of their belief, the utter certainty that they have become someone else, their mind alters their physiology** in measurable and amazing ways. Their eyes actually change color, physical marks disappear and reappear, and even diseases such as diabetes or high blood pressure come and go. All of this is based on a patient's belief as to which personality—which *belief*—is being manifested.

On a less sensational yet just as powerful level, what transformations have occurred in your life when you've changed a belief?

76

What's the secret of success? Often we assume that it's genius. **Yet I believe that true genius is the ability to marshal our most potent resources simply by putting ourselves in a state of absolute certainty.**

Billionaire Bill Gates' career was launched when as a college student at Harvard he promised to deliver software he hadn't developed yet for a computer he'd never seen! Because of his sense of certainty (which was completely unfounded), he was able to tap all the resources he needed to successfully co-design the software and begin to build his fortune.

Clearly, we are more likely to succeed in any arena if we are not only committed to achieving a result, but also absolutely certain we can do so. *How often do you train yourself to feel this empowering emotion?*

77

Perhaps Einstein said it best: "Imagination is more powerful than knowledge." **Time and again it's been proven that our brains cannot tell the difference between something we vividly imagine and something we actually experience.**

Once you understand this, it can transform your life. For example, many people are afraid to try something just because they've never done it before. Yet the very foundation of leaders' success is that, despite past experiences to the contrary, they repeatedly imagine obtaining their desired results. In this way they forge the sense of certainty that guides them to tap into their true potential.

Do you have a goal that excites you but involves doing something you've never done before? When would now be a good time to start imagining yourself succeeding?

78

Most people who say, "Be realistic," are living in fear. Often because of past disappointments and their own perceived failures they are afraid of being let down again. The limiting beliefs they've developed to protect themselves cause them to hesitate, shy away from risk, and avoid giving their all; consequently, they get limited results.

Great leaders are rarely "realistic" by other people's standards. They are, however, accurate and intelligent. Mahatma Gandhi believed he could gain autonomy for India by peacefully, nonviolently opposing Great Britain, something that had never been done before. He wasn't being realistic, but he certainly proved to be accurate.

Which so-called realistic beliefs should you shun? What are some exciting, new, unrealistic but entirely possible expectations you can embrace?

79

If you're going to make a mistake, often it's better to err on the side of *over*estimating your capabilities. Why? Your success may depend on it. One of the differences between pessimists and optimists is that, after attempting to learn a new skill, pessimists generally assess their performance accurately, while optimists view their behavior as more effective than it actually was.

As a result, pessimists give up, seeing no intelligent reason to continue a fruitless endeavor. **Yet optimists' positive perceptions provide them with the emotional support and drive to persist and eventually master the skill.** Thus seemingly unrealistic evaluations become a reflection of actual skill.

Remember, the past does not equal the future. *What is the first small step you could take toward the dream you once thought was impossible?*

80

How we deal with adversity shapes our lives more than almost anything else. **Achievers usually see problems as transitory,** while those who fail usually see even the smallest problems as everlasting. Adopting the latter mind-set is the first step into the trap of what Dr. Martin Seligman calls *learned helplessness,* which is caused by the following three perceptions:

1) The problem is *permanent* (rather than temporary).
2) The problem is *pervasive* (instead of affecting only one area).
3) The problem is *personal,* evidence that something is wrong with us (rather than an opportunity to learn).

For the next few days, we'll concentrate on the antidotes to these debilitating beliefs. *For today, remember "This, too, shall pass" to counter the first belief. If you keep persisting, you will find a way.*

81

The ability to keep problems in perspective enables achievers to avoid falling prey to the "pervasive problem" mind-set. Instead of saying, "Because I overeat, my whole life is destroyed," they might say, "I have a bit of a challenge with my eating habits," and focus on how to improve their behavior. On the other hand, those who believe their problems are pervasive figure that because they've failed to achieve in one area, *they are failures*—a generalization that leaves them feeling completely helpless.

To overcome the false belief that a problem is all-encompassing, you must take control of some part of it immediately. It doesn't matter whether you tackle even the smallest part of the problem; *just get started now.*

82

Optimists see failures as learning experiences, as challenges to modify their approach. Pessimists take failures personally, interpreting them as evidence of some deep-seated character flaw. Because their identity is tied so closely to the problem, they feel overwhelmed. After all, how can they change their entire lives in one stroke?

Avoid this belief of the problem being "personal" at all costs. Begin to use problems as valuable feedback to help you steer a straighter course toward your destiny, and be grateful for these gifts.

83

All personal breakthroughs begin with a change in beliefs. How do you replace limiting beliefs? The most effective way is to destabilize your old belief—shake your certainty—by questioning it.

Remember that your brain is always trying to move you away from pain, so think about all the negative consequences this belief has caused. *Ask yourself:*

1) As I reconsider it, what's actually silly, ridiculous, or stupid about this belief?

2) What has this belief already cost me? How has it limited me in the past?

3) What could it cost me in the future if I don't change now?

Answering these types of questions will help you associate painful feelings to the old, undesired belief and provide you with the opportunity to replace it with an empowering one.

84

In order to be happy, human beings must feel they are continuing to grow. And in order to succeed in today's business world, organizations must constantly be improving. Clearly, we must adopt the concept of continuous improvement as a daily principle rather than as a goal to be pursued only occasionally.

In Japan they have a name for this: *kaizen,* which means to focus on constantly improving the quality of products and services. **I propose that we Americans commit ourselves to the process of *C*onstant *A*nd *N*ever-ending *I*mprovement, or CANI!™** If we habitually focus on how to improve things that are already great, can you see how this spirit can transform our organizations, families, and communities?

How could you put the philosophy of CANI! into practice immediately?

85

The only true security in life comes from knowing that every single day you are improving yourself in some way. **I don't worry about maintaining the quality of my life, because every day I work on *improving* it.**

86

One of the secrets of legendary NBA coach Pat Riley's success is his commitment to gradual, consistent improvement. In 1986 he was faced with a major challenge: his team thought they'd played their best, but the championship had still eluded them the year before. To inspire them to move to the next level, he convinced them that if each enhanced their performance by a mere 1 percent in five key areas, it would make all the difference.

The genius of this plan was its simplicity: Everyone *felt certain* they could achieve it. Each player had only to dedicate himself to a 5 percent increase, but, multiplied by 12 players, it produced a 60 percent improvement for the team—their best season ever!

What could you accomplish with some small but steady improvements?

87

What beliefs guide your thoughts, decisions, and actions every day? *Do this exercise to realize how powerfully your beliefs affect you.*

1) At the top of one piece of paper, write, "Empowering Beliefs." At the top of another, write, "Disempowering Beliefs."

2) For the next ten minutes, list all your beliefs on these two pages. Write down everything that comes to your mind.

3) As you brainstorm, include both global and more specific beliefs. Make sure you include if-then beliefs such as "If I consistently give my all, then I will succeed," or "If I'm totally passionate with this person, then I'll scare them away."

88

One of the most effective ways to improve your life is simply to **identify and reinforce any beliefs you have that will move you in the direction of your dreams.**

1) Review the list you made of your empowering and disempowering beliefs (No. 87 of this book); circle the three most empowering ones.

2) Precisely how do these beliefs empower you? In what ways do they strengthen your character or enhance the quality of your life? If they were even stronger, how could they have an even greater positive influence?

3) Create convictions out of any or all of these empowering beliefs. Generate the unstoppable certainty that will guide your behavior in the direction you want to go. Now, start acting on your convictions!

89

It's time to get rid of beliefs **that no longer serve you!**

1) Pick two of your most disempowering beliefs.

2) Knock the legs of certainty out from under them by asking: How is this belief ridiculous or absurd? Was the person I learned this belief from the best role model? If I don't let go of this belief what will it ultimately cost me emotionally? physically? financially? in my relationships? What will it cost my family and loved ones?

3) Visualize the negative consequences these beliefs carry with them. Decide, once and for all, that you're no longer willing to pay the price.

4) Write down two new beliefs to replace the old ones.

5) Reinforce your new, empowering beliefs by visualizing and anticipating the immeasurable benefits they will yield.

90

The power of expectation in enhancing performance is well documented and has been called the Pygmalion Effect. In one study, teachers were told that **certain students in their classes were gifted and needed to be constantly challenged in order to excel.** The teachers complied and, not surprisingly, these same students became top achievers. However, unbeknownst to them all, the students identified as gifted hadn't actually demonstrated higher intelligence prior to the study. Some, in fact, had previously been labeled poor students. What made the difference? Their newfound sense of certainty that they were superior (instilled by a teacher's "false" belief)!

Can you see the importance of your beliefs about yourself and other people? *What could you accomplish if only you had the faith to tap your vast potential?*

QUESTIONS ARE THE ANSWER

QUESTIONS

●

"The important thing is not to stop questioning. Curiosity has its own reason for existing. One cannot help but be in awe when he contemplates the mysteries of eternity, of life, of the marvelous structure of reality. It is enough if one tries merely to comprehend a little of this mystery every day. Never lose a holy curiosity."

—ALBERT EINSTEIN

91

Questions are the laser of human consciousness. Use their power to cut through any obstacle or challenge.

92

What's the primary difference between people who are successful and those who aren't? **Quite simply, successful people are those who have asked better questions and, as a result, gotten better answers.** When the automobile was in its infancy, hundreds of people tinkered with building them, but Henry Ford stood apart by asking, "How can I mass-produce such a machine?" Millions in Eastern Europe chafed under the iron yoke of communism, but Lech Walesa had the courage to ask, "How can I raise the standard of living for all working men and women?"

If you were to let your imagination run wild, where might your questions lead you?

93

Do you agree or disagree with the following statement? *Thinking is nothing but the process of asking and answering questions.* In order to respond either way, didn't you have to ask yourself a question such as "Is that really true?" or "Do I agree with what he is saying?"

Most of our thought processes—from evaluating ("How is that so?") to imagining ("What is possible?") to deciding ("What shall I do?")—involve asking and answering questions. **Therefore, if we want to change the quality of our lives, we must change what we habitually ask of ourselves and others.**

94

Kids are the all-time champions of questioning. What could you gain by imitating the innocence and curiosity of children who are completely determined to get an answer?

My life's work is the result of **asking questions:** What makes people do what they do? What has enabled certain people to achieve success with seemingly fewer resources than some who have failed? How can we duplicate their results? How can we produce change more easily and quickly than ever before? How can we improve the quality of life for all people?

What are the primary questions that are currently shaping your life?

96

Quality questions create a quality life. Businesses succeed when their decision makers ask the right questions about product lines or markets or strategic planning. Relationships flourish when people ask the right questions about where potential conflicts exist and how to support each other rather than tearing each other down. Communities benefit when leaders ask the right questions about what is most important and how citizens can work together toward shared goals.

For whatever area of your life you want to improve, there are questions you can ask that will provide you with answers—*solutions*—that can catapult you and those you love to a higher level of success and enjoyment. *Do you need to ask questions about quality? commitment? contribution?*

97

Questions set off a processional effect that has an impact beyond our imagining. Questioning our limitations is what tears down the walls—in business, in relationships, between countries. **All human progress is preceded by new questions.**

What new question could you ask yourself to come up with new answers that can improve your life today?

98

There is no question that the capacity of our brains is phenomenal. **In fact, it would take two buildings the size of the World Trade Center to house the storage capacity of your brain.** Yet without an understanding of how to retrieve and use all that's been stored, this potential is useless. What enables you to get anything you want from your personal data banks? The commanding power of asking questions. Often our failure to utilize our experiences is not a memory failure as much as it is a failure to ask the questions that tap into our abilities.

99

Your mental computer is always ready to serve you, and whatever question you give it, it will surely come up with an answer. If you ask a lousy question like "Why do I keep screwing up?" you'll get a lousy answer. On the other hand, when you ask a much more useful question such as "How can I use this?" it automatically leads you in the direction of solutions.

New answers come from new questions. *What is an empowering question you could ask yourself or someone you love right now?*

100

The power of asking brilliant questions is illustrated by my good friend W. Mitchell. After an accident in which his entire body was burned and he lost the use of his legs, he refused to feel sorry for himself. "What do I still have?" he asked. **"What am I capable of now, even more so than before?** Because of this incident, what will I be able to contribute to others?"

In the hospital he met a nurse named Annie and was instantly attracted to her. With his body burned beyond recognition and paralyzed from the waist down, he had the remarkable audacity to ask himself, "How could I get a date with her?" Soon they were married.

If the possibility of failure or rejection were not a consideration, what questions could you be asking yourself right now?

101

When people are reluctant to commit to a romantic relationship, could it be that they are asking questions that create doubt, such as "What if there's somebody even better out there? What if I commit myself now and miss out?" This would keep them from being able to enjoy what they already have.

What if they asked these questions instead: **"How did I get so lucky to have you in my life?"** "What do I love the most about you?" "How much richer will our lives be as a result of our relationship?"

What questions could you ask of yourself and your mate that would make the two of you feel like the luckiest people on earth?

102

No matter what we've already achieved, there will be times when we come up against roadblocks to personal and professional progress. The question is not whether you're going to have problems, but how you're going to deal with them when they come up. *Use this checklist to change your state and open yourself up to solutions.*

THE PROBLEM-SOLVING QUESTIONS

1) What is great about this problem?
2) What is not perfect yet?
3) What am I willing to do to make it the way I want it?
4) What am I willing to no longer do in order to make it the way I want it?
5) How can I enjoy the process while I do what is necessary to make it the way I want it?

103

What enabled Donald Trump to build his fortune in real estate? Surely one key must have been his evaluation procedure. In assessing any property that seemed to offer tremendous potential for economic gain, he would ask, "What's the downside? What's the worst that could happen, and can I handle it?" If he knew he could manage the worst-case scenario, then he'd proceed with the deal because the upside would take care of itself.

When Trump began to suffer setbacks, observers noted that he had begun to believe he was invincible and had dispensed with his downside questions. **Remember, it's not only the questions you ask, but the questions you fail to ask, that shape your destiny.**

104

The questions you ask consistently will create either enervation or enjoyment, indignation or inspiration, misery or magic. **Ask the questions that will uplift your spirit and push you along the path of human excellence.**

105

If you have repeatedly tried and failed to lose weight, could it be that you were asking yourself the wrong questions? Questions like "What will fill me up?" or "What's the sweetest, richest food I can get away with?"

What if you were to ask instead, "What would really nourish me?" "What light, delicious dish can I eat that would give me energy?" "Will this cleanse me or clog me?" And, if you're tempted to binge: "If I eat this, what will I have to give up in order to still achieve my goals? What's the ultimate price I'll pay if I indulge now?"

A single change in the habitual questions you ask yourself can and will profoundly change the quality of your life.

106

Questions immediately change what we're focusing on and therefore how we feel. **Don't you have treasured moments in your life that, if you just focused on them again, you'd immediately feel wonderful?** Perhaps it was the day you moved out on your own, the birth of your first child, or a conversation with a friend that helped give you the confidence to shoot for the stars. Questions such as "What can I be grateful for?" and "What's wonderful in my life right now?" guide us to remember these moments, allowing us not only to feel good about our lives, but also to contribute more to those around us.

107

There's a big difference between an affirmation and a question. You can repeat affirmations like "I'm happy, I'm happy, I'm happy" all day long, but it won't produce the same state of certainty as consistently asking an empowering question like **"What am I happy about now? What *could* I be happy about now if I wanted to be? How would that make me feel?"** Rather than merely pumping you up, questions direct your focus and get you to come up with real and compelling reasons to feel the emotion. Thus, instead of stating a mere affirmation, you'll experience an actual emotional state change—something real, something that will last.

108

How do you immediately improve your life? By discovering and modeling the habitual questions of people you respect. If you find someone who's extremely happy, I can guarantee you there's one reason: this person focuses relentlessly on whatever makes him or her happy, and continually asks questions about how to become even happier. People who do well financially ask different questions as they look at investments than people who produce meager rewards.

A new level of success in any area of your life is as close as a new question that you've modeled from someone who's already experiencing that which you desire. Remember, ask and you shall receive!

109

One of the main ingredients of success is the openness to receive answers. Back when Walt Disney was creating his Magic Kingdom, he had a unique way of requesting input. He'd designate an entire wall to display all the stages of a project, and everyone in his organization was invited to post their answers to the question "How can we improve this?" Thus Disney gained access to the combined resources of a creative army, producing results commensurate with that quality of input.

You don't have to be at the helm of a leading organization to benefit from this tool. *How could you cast your focus in new directions?* What people with whom you interact daily could provide you with a wealth of resources—if only you asked?

110

The answers we receive depend upon the questions we're willing to ask. It's all a matter of discovering the particular questions that will help you to access more resourceful states. For example, if learning and progress are important to you, then a question such as **"How can I use this situation to do even better in the future?"** will be most effective in breaking a negative emotional pattern.

With especially difficult upsets, you might ask, "Ten years from now, will this really even matter?"

To deal with relationship upsets, asking a question such as "What else could be affecting this person, and how can I help?" would be the quickest way to resolve your differences and express your compassion.

111

Human beings are marvelous "deletion creatures." Of all the things we could be noticing at any given time, there is only a small number we can consciously focus on.

By asking a question, either of yourself or of someone else, you can instantly change focus. For instance, a question like "Have you ever thought about the impact we're going to have because of what we've created here?" can cause a co-worker or team member to delete immediately all the troublesome details of a project and to begin focusing instead on all the long-term benefits.

Is there someone you know who could really benefit from this type of boost?

112

Whatever we look for we'll find. To prove this to yourself, try an experiment. *Wherever you are right now, take a minute to look at your surroundings, then ask yourself, "What do I see that's brown?"* Take note of everything you see that's this color.

Next, close your eyes. Then recall everything that's... *green.* This will probably be difficult enough if you're already acquainted with your surroundings, but if you're in an unfamiliar area, it will definitely be a challenge! You'll easily remember everything that's brown, but most likely draw blanks on anything that's green.

To conclude, open your eyes and notice everything that's green. Chances are that anything that's green will really pop out at you! **Remember, "Seek and ye shall find."** Be conscious about what you look for.

113

Whether we consider something possible or impossible is often determined by the way we ask questions. The specific words and the order in which they're used can cause us to not even consider certain possibilities —or to take others completely for granted. Asking, "Why do I always sabotage myself?" for example, sets in motion a self-fulfilling prophecy; it presupposes that you do indeed sabotage yourself when that really may not be the case at all.

Learn to turn presupposition to your advantage. Find references to back up new beliefs that empower you. Ask yourself, "How is this experience perfecting my skills?" or "Because of what we've just been through together, how will our relationship be made even stronger?"

114

Questions create answers where seemingly none exist.

Early in my career, an associate embezzled a large sum of money. **Rather than filing bankruptcy (as I was repeatedly counseled), I asked myself, "How can I turn this around?** How can I cause my company to have even more impact than before? How can I help people even while I sleep?" These questions enabled me to create a franchise division and a highly successful series of television infomercials that have benefited the lives of millions of people.

If you don't get the answers you want at first, do you give up? Or do you keep asking, in as many ways as you have to, to get the answers you need?

115

Create a daily success ritual for yourself. Every morning, come up with at least two or three answers to each of the following questions, basking in the positive emotions they inspire. If you have difficulty with an answer, simply add "could." For example, if you can't answer the question "What am I most happy about in my life right now?" ask, "What *could* I be most happy about in my life right now if I wanted to?"

THE MORNING POWER QUESTIONS

1) What am I happy about in my life right now? What about that makes me happy? How does that make me feel?

2) What am I excited about in my life right now? What about that makes me excited? How does that make me feel?

116

THE MORNING POWER QUESTIONS (Continued)

3) What am I proud about in my life right now? What about that makes me proud? How does that make me feel?

4) What am I grateful about in my life right now? What about that makes me grateful? How does that make me feel?

5) What am I enjoying most in my life right now? What about that do I enjoy? How does that make me feel?

6) What am I committed to in my life right now? What about that makes me committed? How does that make me feel?

7) Who do I love? Who loves me? What about that makes me loving? How does that make me feel?

Next you'll learn how to make this daily success ritual even more effective.

117

An excellent follow-up to the Morning Power Questions is the three Evening Power Questions, a checklist designed to put the events of your day in perspective. Since you've been asking yourself questions all day, why not ask ones that will put you in a great state before you drop off to sleep?

THE EVENING POWER QUESTIONS

1) What have I given today? In what ways have I been a contributor?
2) What did I learn today? What new distinctions have I made?
3) How has today enhanced the quality of my life? How can I use today as an investment in my future?
4) (Optional: Repeat the Morning Power Questions.)

118

The only thing that limits your questions is your belief about what is possible. A core belief that has positively shaped my destiny is that **if I continue to ask any question, I will certainly receive an answer.** Just as in a *Jeopardy!* game, every answer is already there—all you have to do is come up with the right question.

119

What questions would be useful for you to ask yourself on a regular basis? Two of my favorites are at once the simplest and most powerful in helping me overcome challenges: **"What's great about this?" and "How can I use this?"** Asking the first question disrupts negative momentum and reminds me that we can choose to attach any meaning whatsoever to an experience. Asking the second question focuses me on the "how" rather than the "why," on solutions and benefits rather than the unanswerable.

What two questions could you start using to change your states and access your resources? Add these to your Morning Power Questions so that they become an integral part of your daily ritual for success.

120

A simple question that can make a huge difference was suggested to me by Leo Buscaglia, who has contributed so much in the arena of human relations. When he was young, Leo's father asked him every night, **"What have you learned today?"** The boy knew he had to have an answer—and a good one. If he hadn't learned anything interesting in school that day, he'd scurry for the encyclopedia. Decades later, Leo still won't go to bed until he's learned something new and valuable for the day.

How could your life or your children's lives be immeasurably enhanced by adding this question, or one like it, to your daily routine? In what ways could you make this process as fundamental as eating or sleeping?

121

At some point you must stop asking questions and start taking action. Questions such as "What is my life really about?" "What am I most committed to?" and "Why am I here?" are incredibly powerful, but **if you agonize over getting the perfect answer, you won't get very far.** The gut-level response to any question is often the one that should be trusted and acted upon. So, in order to produce results, simply decide what's most important to you—at least in the moment—and use your personal power to follow through and begin transforming the quality of your life.

GET THE kNACk OF CHANGE

THE SCIENCE OF
SUCCESS CONDITIONING

●

*"Habit is either the best of servants or
the worst of masters."*

—NATHANIEL EMMONS

122

I've always prided myself on my ability to produce lasting changes in almost anyone. I had a rude awakening one day, though, when a man I'd helped years before to quit smoking approached me, pulled a cigarette pack from his pocket, and said, "You failed!"

"What do you mean?" I asked, curious to know what had happened.

"After our session, I didn't smoke for two and a half years. But then one day when I got stressed, I lit up, and I've been smoking ever since. It's all your fault! You didn't program me properly!"

Although his communication was less than elegant, this man gave me an incredible gift. He reminded me that **we must take personal responsibility for our change.** No one can "program" you. You must *condition* yourself.

123

Any change we make will be only temporary unless we make ourselves —no one or nothing else—responsible for our own change. Specifically, we must adopt these three core beliefs:

1) It <u>must</u> change. Believing that we *should* change is not enough.
2) I <u>must</u> change it. Others can coach me, but I'm responsible.
3) I <u>can</u> change it. I created what I'm experiencing; therefore, I can change it.

124

What really makes change happen? It happens when we alter in our nervous system the sensations we link to an experience.

As long as cigarettes give you feelings of pleasure, you'll be drawn to them. It's only when you associate cigarettes with disgust, "ashtray mouth," and death that lasting change will actually occur.

Though we'd like to deny it, **what usually drives our behavior is gut reaction, not intellectual calculation.** You may understand that chocolate is unhealthy, yet do you still eat it? Why? Because you're not driven so much by what you intellectually know, but instead by what you've learned to link pain and pleasure to *in your nervous system.* It's our *neuro-associations*—the associations we've established in our nervous systems—that determine what we'll do.

125

Why don't most attempts at breaking a habit work? Because we address the symptoms of the problem—by dieting, going cold turkey, or cutting up the credit cards—but if we don't eliminate its *cause*, it will resurface.

The technology I've developed—Neuro-Associative Conditioning™ (NAC)—is a simple yet powerful six-step strategy for producing lasting change:

1) State clearly what you really want. Most people focus on what they don't want.

2) Get leverage. Make change a must.

3) Interrupt the limiting pattern. Break the habit's "hold" on you.

4) Create a new, empowering alternative. You can't just stop a behavior or an emotion; you must replace it.

5) Condition it—until it's a new habit.

6) Test it. Make sure it works!

126

What prevents us from making a change? **Some of our beliefs, both personal and cultural, can hold us back.**

Many people don't believe they can make a change merely because previous attempts have failed. Or they might think change has to be a long, painful process; if not, they argue, then why haven't they changed already? Furthermore, if you resolve a problem you've been dealing with for years in a matter of minutes, you have to face your friends and family: they might ask, "If it was that easy, why did we waste time worrying about you?" With all these negative "incentives," we've learned to take a long time so people can "appreciate" our change.

Shake off this cultural hypnosis and realize that new actions will produce new results now.

127

We've all been taught that quick shifts—in behavior, belief, or emotion —can mean that we're hypocritical, fickle, or unstable. Conversely, people considered consistent are labeled "trustworthy," "solid," "true-blue." Yet all of this creates tremendous external pressure to preserve the status quo and continue to do exactly what is expected of us.

Just realize that if you can instantly create a problem, you can just as quickly and easily create a solution! If you think about it, when someone seems to take a long time to change, has it really taken that long to change—or just that long to get to the point where change is a must?

To create change quickly, the first belief you must adopt is that you can change virtually anything <u>now</u>.

128

There's nothing wrong with you. **You're not broken. You don't need to be "fixed."** If you constantly avoid rejection, your brain is simply doing an effective job of protecting you from pain. But completely avoiding the opposite sex also produces pain! To create a new behavior, you must simply "rewire" yourself. The resources you need to change anything in your life are within you right now, just waiting to be tapped.

If you wish to make an improvement in some area of your life, either in your behavior or emotions, identify it now and use the rest of this section to help you achieve what you want.

129

NAC MASTER STEP #1

Decide what you really want **and determine what's preventing you from having it now.**

Remember that we get whatever we focus on. Rather than dwelling on what you don't want, clearly articulate what you *do* want. For example, instead of making it your goal to "stop smoking," decide that you want to "be more healthy, vibrant, and alive than ever before." The more specific you are, the more power you will have to rapidly achieve your goal.

Once you've decided what you want, identify any obstacles you might face, such as the anticipated pain that might occur as a result of changing.

What do you desire? What is preventing you from having it now?

130

Have you ever noticed how, when people get injured and are waited on hand and foot, sometimes their injuries don't heal as quickly? Although what they really want is to recover from the injury, the pleasure of receiving all that loving attention, and the permission to relax, may unconsciously delay or prevent their healing. **When people derive a secondary benefit from the very painful behavior or emotion they're trying to change, this is called *secondary gain*.** This need to preserve the secondary benefit is often one of the greatest inhibitors of lasting change.

What hidden benefits might you derive from a behavior you know you should change? How attractive are they when weighed against the pain you know this behavior has caused you in the past, present, and future?

131

NAC MASTER STEP #2

Get leverage: **Associate massive pain to not changing now and immense pleasure to immediately making the change.** *Ask:*

1) What will this behavior (or emotion) cost me if I don't change?
2) What will I miss out on in my life if I don't make this shift?
3) What is the old behavior already costing me mentally? emotionally? physically? financially? spiritually?
4) How does this affect my career? loved ones?

Vividly imagine and experience the pleasurable effects of changing now. Ask:

1) When I do change, how will that make me feel about myself?
2) What kind of momentum will I create by making this change?
3) How will my family and friends feel?
4) How happy will I be?
5) *Don't I deserve these benefits now?*

132

He'd tried almost everything to quit smoking. Nothing worked until his six-year-old daughter walked into the room crying, "Daddy, please stop killing yourself! I want you to be there...*when I get married!*" No amount of reasoning could convince her that smoking wouldn't kill him ... His cigarettes went out the door that day, and he hasn't smoked since. Sometimes your own pain isn't enough to make a change, but the pain of those you love can provide powerful leverage.

If you've tried and failed to make a shift, the missing ingredient was probably *leverage.* Unless you get yourself to the point where change is an absolute must, you'll probably continue putting it off. But with strong enough reasons—the right leverage—you'll be compelled to act.

133

Want a fail-safe strategy for shedding unwanted pounds? How about this idea:

Get a weight-loss buddy and promise him or her and a group of other friends that you will begin a strict regimen of healthy foods and enjoyable exercise. Further commit to them that if you break your promise, you will eat a whole can of Alpo dog food.

The woman who shared this with me told me that she and her friend kept their cans in plain view at all times (no pun intended!) to remind them of their commitment. When they started to feel hunger pangs or consider skipping exercise, they'd pick up the can and read the label. Such appetizing ingredients as "horsemeat chunks" helped them achieve their goals without a hitch!

134

NAC MASTER STEP #3

Interrupt the limiting pattern.

Have you ever seen a fly trapped in a room? Desperately seeking an exit, it repeatedly smacks itself against the nearest window.

Have you ever noticed people doing something a lot like this? They may have plenty of motivation, but if they keep doing what doesn't work, they'll never achieve their goal. It's like the spouse or parent who constantly nags, yet to no avail—or even to contrary results.

Interrupt limiting patterns by doing something unexpected. If you nag, catch yourself mid-sentence, drop to your knees, and flash...a smile! Walk over, give 'em a hug, and tell them how much you love them.

What are some fun, playful ways you can interrupt a limiting pattern?

135

To create a new pattern of thinking, feeling, or behaving, you must first interrupt the old pattern. To visualize this, think of a compact disc. Why does it play the same music every time? Because there's an invisible pattern cut into it.

Just as it's futile to insert a new CD while another one is still playing, **it's a waste of time trying to establish a new behavioral/emotional pattern with the old pattern still entrenched.** Instead, the minute you indulge in this pattern, interrupt it with as many crazy, bizarre, and fun things you can. It's like hearing a song you don't ever want to listen to again, ejecting the disc, and vigorously scratching its surface until you're certain you'll never be able to hear this "song" again.

136

The reason it's often difficult to change a pattern (emotional or behavioral) is that it's literally "wired" into you. One researcher proved this by moving a monkey's finger back and forth and monitoring the resulting connections between nerve cells in the brain as they were made. With repeated movement, he noted that the thread of connection strengthened, and after he'd moved the animal's finger hundreds of times they bound together to form an irresistible pathway. Now "wired" for this behavior, the monkey continued flexing its finger of its own accord even after the conditioning stopped.

Many of us—through overuse—have trained ourselves to fly off the handle . . . worry ourselves sick . . . feel insecure . . . abuse alcohol.

What positive reflexes can you strengthen through repetition?

137

Are there unconscious patterns shaping your life? Many people, for example, repeat the same daily motions to get to work: taking the same freeway, the same exit, etc. We train our brains and bodies to function in a specific pattern until it becomes a habit. What happens on the one day we need to take a different exit? Most of us, out of our conditioning, drive right past it.

In other areas of our lives, we have emotional or behavioral patterns that are just as ingrained. Does anyone you know have a habit of getting angry, frustrated, or overwhelmed? Maybe it's time you trained yourself to feel happy, excited, or grateful. Sound difficult? It's as easy as playfully interrupting your old emotional pattern and replacing it with a pleasurable one.

138

Whatever you fail to use you lose. An easy way to interrupt a limiting pattern is simply to avoid indulging in it. A nerve pathway (neuro-association) unused will gradually atrophy. Beware, however: this works for both the negative and the positive.... **Courage unused diminishes; commitment unexercised wanes; passion unexpressed dissipates.**

Right now, make a decision to do something that causes you to utilize one of your richest and most empowering emotions. Remember, the more you use something, the stronger it becomes. Our emotional muscles must be exercised, not only to produce results, but to keep us in a healthy and prepared state.

139

NAC MASTER STEP #4

Create a new, empowering alternative.

A study of reformed drug abusers found there were different relapse rates for different individuals. Those who were forced externally to give up their drug abuse resumed it immediately upon being released from jail. Those who were internally motivated to quit managed to abstain for about two years. Those who replaced their addictions with new alternatives—such as focusing on religion, developing a new work skill—generally went eight or more years without backsliding, and the majority never abused drugs again.

Most people's attempts at change are only temporary because they fail to find an alternative way of getting out of pain and into pleasure. Old patterns must be *replaced,* not just eliminated.

140

NAC MASTER STEP #5

Condition the new pattern **until it's consistent.**

I got a real education in conditioning one day as I watched a piano tuner working on our new baby grand. When I asked him for the bill, he said he'd let us know on his next visit. "You mean you're not done?" I asked. Patiently he explained that the piano strings were strong and that, in order to keep them at the perfect level of tension, they'd have to be consistently *conditioned* to stay at that level.

This is exactly what we must do to create lasting change. We must condition our nervous systems to succeed not just once, but consistently. After all, you wouldn't go to just one aerobics class and proclaim, "Now I'm healthy for life!"

141

Remember the monkey that, through consistent use of its finger, literally created a neural connection that drove it to continually flex it? Researchers proved that if they emotionally excited the animal while training it, the neural connection was strengthened and intensified with fewer repetitions. If you rehearse a new behavior by imagining it or practicing it regularly with emotional intensity (e.g., excitement, passion) you'll establish a new "neural highway" to pleasure. This kind of conditioning ensures that you automatically feel compelled to drive along your new "route" (emotional/behavioral pattern).

Remember, it's important to reinforce the new pattern of behavior by immediately rewarding yourself (or someone you're helping) whenever you use it. Any pattern of thinking, feeling, or behavior that is consistently reinforced will become a habit.

142

The irresistible power of conditioning is graphically illustrated by Boston Celtics great Larry Bird. When he was hired to star in a soft-drink commercial, the script called for him to miss a shot. **He made nine baskets in a row before he could bring himself to miss!** He had been so conditioned to put that ball through the hoop that it took all of his concentration and a good deal of practice to flub even one. No doubt there is a part of Larry Bird's brain that is a virtual neural superhighway to the sequence of motions required to sink a basket.

Know that we can condition any behavior if we do it with enough repetition and emotional intensity.

143

A fundamental law of conditioning is that any pattern that is continually reinforced will become an automatic and conditioned response. **Anything we fail to reinforce will eventually dissipate.**

What rewards—mental, emotional, physical—could you give yourself to create the new positive habits you desire?

144

Can you teach a chicken to dance? Amazingly, yes, because **all animals—and humans—have variable behavior.**

The trainers' secret is to watch the chicken closely. Whenever it naturally moves in the direction they want, they immediately reinforce it with a bit of food. At this point the chicken doesn't know why it's been fed, but each time it moves in the direction the trainers want, they reward/reinforce it. Eventually the chicken learns to turn in the desired directions, and a sequence of these form a dance.

Obviously people are more complex than chickens. Yet have you been trained to behave a certain way at work or in school? *How can you use this training principle to help yourself, your employees, or your children create successful habits?*

145

CONDITIONING TECHNIQUE #1

Impeccable timing is absolutely critical **to effective conditioning.** For reinforcement to work, it must happen at the exact moment the person does something you want. If too much time passes before the behavior is reinforced, either negatively or positively, then the connection is made intellectually, but not emotionally in the nervous system.

For example, people who are ticketed for parking in a handicapped zone may suffer some inconvenience later. But since they don't have to pay the fine for several weeks, repeat offenders tend not to link much pain to the behavior. I can guarantee you, though, that if every time they parked in a handicapped zone, their car immediately exploded, not only would their pattern be broken but a new pattern would be instantly installed!

<u>146</u>

CONDITIONING TECHNIQUE #1 EXERCISE

Make a list of pleasurable rewards you can give yourself immediately when you do the "right things." Then set up a specific situation in which you consciously reinforce yourself using one of these rewards.

CONDITIONING TECHNIQUE #2

Consistency of reinforcement is very important when you're first conditioning a new pattern. *Every time* you perform the desired behavior (for example, you get up from the table before you're full, or you turn down someone's offer of a cigarette), reward yourself immediately.

147

CONDITIONING TECHNIQUE #3

Animal trainers know that if you keep feeding a dolphin every single time it jumps, pretty soon it won't jump unless you feed it. Worse yet, it may become satiated and not even bother jumping at all.

You and I are no different—nor are our children, business associates, or anyone else we deal with. If you reinforce somebody every single time, it soon becomes boring. **Once a pattern of behavior is established, the tool of *variable reinforcement* is far more effective for maintaining it.** So, after about a month of consistent rewards for a new behavior, taper off. *Instead, reward yourself or others spontaneously!*

148

Variable reinforcement is one of the most powerful conditioning tools
on the planet. Consider, for example, the allure of gambling for some
people. If they were to win every time, it'd be exciting at first, but soon
it would become too much like work (i.e., pull the handle all day and get
paid for it!). The drama of being uncertain as to whether you will be
rewarded or not excites the nervous system, increasing the intensity of
pleasure at the moment of reward into a powerful conditioning experience. This is the high that addicts people. Likewise, if you stop smoking
then give yourself the "reward" of just one cigarette, you induce the
power of variable reinforcement and actually intensify your addiction. *At
all costs, avoid falling into this trap.*

149

CONDITIONING TECHNIQUE #4

To create lasting change, **it is most effective to combine two techniques:**

1) Reward yourself at set intervals for specific actions (this is known as "fixed schedule" reinforcement). For example, dolphins being trained to jump consistently ten times are rewarded on the tenth jump—*every time.* However, to ensure that they don't learn to give their best effort only on the tenth jump, other jumps are rewarded randomly. Thus the dolphin always jumps high because of the "exciting possibility" of reward.

2) Therefore, to effectively reinforce yourself or others, be sure to include some special surprise for extraordinary efforts.

Remember how great it felt the last time you got an unexpected bonus at work? special recognition at school? a surprise weekend getaway with your lover?

150

CONDITIONING TECHNIQUE #5

One of the most valuable training tools, whether of dolphins or people, is the *jackpot.* Occasionally, if a dolphin isn't performing well, a trainer will give it fish anyway, apparently for no good reason. Frequently this type of surprise stimulates the dolphin to begin jumping again.

The next time you or someone else become overwhelmed, maybe what's needed is a jackpot—some special form of treatment the person didn't have to work for, but that is just enough to interrupt the current uninspired pattern of behavior and "jump-start" the recipient into trying something new. Just as important, giving a larger reward than someone expects for excellent behavior will produce extraordinary efforts in the future.

Do you know someone who either needs or deserves to hit the jackpot today?

NAC MASTER STEP #6

Test it!

Use the following to double-check that you've taken each of the five preceding steps correctly:

1) Make certain that when you think of your old pattern of feeling or behaving, you immediately associate intense pain to it.

2) Be sure pleasure is fully associated with the new pattern: When you think of your new behavior or feelings, do you feel pleasure instead of pain?

3) Make certain that this new behavior is consistent with how you want to live your life. Is it aligned with your goals? your beliefs? your life philosophy?

4) Make sure the benefits of the old pattern have been maintained. For example, if you used to smoke in order to calm yourself or reduce stress, do you have a new, alternative way of accomplishing these things that is just as effective? Will the new behavior still allow you to get the feelings of pleasure you used to get from the old pattern?

5) Imagine yourself behaving in this new way in the future: Picture something that would have triggered you to indulge in your old behavior. Make certain that you automatically use your new pattern instead of the old one.

THE VOCABULARY OF SUCCESS

THE POWER OF TRANSFORMATIONAL VOCABULARY AND GLOBAL METAPHORS

•

*"Words form the thread
on which we string our experiences."*

—ALDOUS HUXLEY

152

Have you ever been deeply moved by a great communicator? Do you still remember the words of a John F. Kennedy, a Winston Churchill, a Martin Luther King, Jr.? Through the power of their words, these men affected not only you and me but entire nations, and even after their deaths they continue to touch others.

Yet do you ever stop to think about the power you have to inspire or depress yourself simply by the words *you* habitually use? Are the words you use uplifting or devastating? **Do they provide hope or despair? One of the greatest discoveries you can make is the power you have to immediately change your experience at a moment's notice simply by consciously selecting the words you use to describe the way you feel.**

153

Words have the power to start wars or create peace, destroy relationships or strengthen them. How we feel about anything is shaped by the meaning we attach to it. The words you consciously or unconsciously select to describe a situation immediately change what it means to you and thus how you feel. If you describe an event to yourself as devastating, will you feel different than if you describe it as a bit disappointing? Is there a difference in emotional intensity between calling something a major problem or a minor challenge? What if you share with me a conviction you have and I tell you you're mistaken? What if I say you're wrong? Worse, what if I choose to use the words, "You're lying"? Will this affect our interaction?

154

Years ago I made a discovery that has changed my life forever. I was in a business meeting with two of my associates, and we all received news that was certain to produce negative consequences. Yet each of us had a different emotional intensity about this. What's more, I couldn't help noticing that we all had different ways of *describing* how we felt. I was "angry," one associate was absolutely "enraged," and the third was merely "annoyed." I remember thinking, what a stupid word to use to describe this situation! I never felt annoyed. Interesting: I never felt this emotion, and I never used that word to describe how I felt. I began to wonder, **if you adopted a new set of words, could you transform your emotional patterns?**

155

Based on the above-described meeting, I made a ten-day commitment to adopt this stupid, silly word—"annoyed"—and to utilize it in any situation where I'd normally say that something made me "angry" or "mad." The results were astonishing. Simply by changing the word I had habitually used to describe my negative feelings, I immediately lowered their intensity. Saying, "This really annoys me," broke my pattern. Soon I adopted other words, such as "You're beginning to *peeve* me." Can you imagine trying to say this to someone you're upset with and keeping a straight face?

Select a word you habitually use to describe your negative feelings, and come up with an alternative word that will break your pattern or at least lower your intensity.

156

When you use a different word for an experience than you ordinarily do, you're attaching a new label to it. It's like pushing a different bio-chemical button: you don't just change intellectually, you change how you feel emotionally. Words are triggering devices. If you doubt this, imagine someone calling you a four-letter word. Most likely this will create a physiological, not just a mental, change in you.

This power to instantly transform emotions, to lower or heighten their intensity, I call Transformational Vocabulary. Simply adjust your habitual vocabulary—the words you consistently use to describe your emotions and sensations—to immediately change how you think, feel, and live. This is one of the simplest yet most powerful tools for changing anyone's life in an instant.

157

Most of us are unconscious in our selection of the words we use to consistently describe our life experience. Often we've adopted words to describe our emotions without ever thinking about the potential impact they'll have on us or others. These words become part of our habitual vocabulary and actually shape the way we feel about our lives.

For example, many people regularly use words like "humiliation" or "depression" to describe virtually any unpleasant experience. Say something they don't appreciate and they're humiliated/depressed. Question their point of view and they're humiliated/depressed. *Everything* humiliates or depresses them, because they attach these words to almost any experience. **It's critical to expand your emotional vocabulary so that the words you select produce the emotional states you desire and deserve.**

158

How important is language in shaping our experience of life? It is absolutely fundamental. **Quite simply, the words we attach to our experience *become* our experience.**

159

Mark Twain once said, "A powerful agent is the right word. Whenever we come upon one of those intensely right words...the resulting effect is physical as well as spiritual, and electrically prompt."

What words have the most powerful effect on you? Are they terms of endearment? epithets? exclamations? exaggerations?

160

Most people's vocabularies consist of only a few thousand words. When you consider that English, the largest language in the world, contains between one-half and three-quarters of a million words, this means that we regularly use only about 2 percent of our language! What's worse is that most people have only about a dozen words, maybe a maximum of 20, to describe their consistent emotions. And of these, usually half—or more—are negative.

How many words do you habitually use to describe the way you feel, either to other people or yourself? How many could you write down right now?

161

Do you ever get nervous if you have to speak in front of a group of people? Does your stomach tense? your breathing quicken? your pulse race? your hands tremble? These sensations prevented Carly Simon from performing live for years. However, other entertainers have discovered how to use them to their advantage. Bruce Springsteen, for instance, labels these exact same physical sensations as "excitement" and considers it a natural and positive part of his preparation to perform. These sensations remind him he's about to have the incredibly powerful experience of entertaining thousands of people. For him, a quickened pulse is not an enemy; it's an ally.

The next time you know you'll be the center of attention, maybe it's time you appreciated this adrenaline rush as excitement rather than fear.

162

Once we put a label on something, we create a corresponding emotion. Nowhere is this truer than with diseases. Studies have shown that diagnoses of cancer and heart disease can often produce panic in patients, leading to helplessness and depression that can actually impair the effectiveness of the immune system. Conversely, studies have proven that if patients are freed or relieved of the depression produced by certain labels and clearly understand what the body needs to do to become healthy, then the immune system often experiences an immediate boost.

Dr. Norman Cousins said it best when we discussed Transformational Vocabulary: **"Words can produce illness; words can kill. Therefore, wise physicians are very careful about the way they communicate."**

Carefully choose the words you use to describe your health.

163

People with impoverished vocabularies live emotionally impoverished lives. People with rich vocabularies have a multi-hued palette of colors with which to paint their life's experience, not only for others, but for themselves as well.

What could you do today to expand your "emotional palette"? What positive and emotionally uplifting words could you add to your habitual vocabulary? If you consistently used these words, how much more enjoyable would your life be?

Who do you know that leads an extraordinarily happy or passionate life? What words do they consistently use to describe their life's experience that you could model, and thereby adopt some of their positive emotional patterns?

164

Have you decided it's high time to use the tool of Transformational Vocabulary to replace your habitually disempowering words with more inspiring ones? Do the following:

1) Write down three words you regularly use when you feel lousy.

2) Put yourself in a playful, maybe even outrageous, state. Brainstorm some new words for breaking your pattern or at least lowering your emotional intensity. Pick words that are so silly, weird, or totally inappropriate that they break your negative momentum and create an instant sense of fun. One of the reasons I now substitute "peeved" or "annoyed" for "angry" is that these words sound so ridiculous. I can't say "peeved" with a straight face.

165

Negative emotional intensity can be lowered **through the use of modifiers and softeners.** In addition to substituting "annoyed" for "angry," why not try some of these phrases: "I'm getting *a bit* peeved." "I'm feeling *a touch* out of sorts." "I'm beginning to get *just a smidge* cranky." "Well, now, isn't that *a tad* inconvenient?"

166

How do you communicate with your children? Often we don't realize the impact our words have upon them. Instead of blurting out, "You're so clumsy!" or "Why can't you be quiet?"—remarks that can powerfully undermine a child's sense of self-worth—**try using humor to break his or her pattern.** For example, you could say, "If you continue on this track, I might start getting a *smidge cranky,*" with a smiling face. Say something that changes not only your child's focus but yours, as well, to pave the way for more appropriate communication and behavior. Then follow up with a suggestion such as, "Honey, if you do this differently, I think you'll get what you really want."

167

Here's how to get leverage on yourself to start using Transformational Vocabulary on a regular basis:

1) Approach three friends and share with them the words or phrases you want to eliminate from your habitual vocabulary, along with the new words or phrases.

2) Monitor yourself for the next ten days. If you catch yourself using the old word, immediately break your pattern with the new word. If you catch yourself automatically using the new word, reward yourself immediately.

3) Your friends are to help you stay on track. Any time they notice you using one of the old words, they are to redirect you. (For example, "Are you mad, or are you just *a little peeved?*" "Are you frustrated or *fascinated?*")

168

Must we always lower the intensity of negative emotions? Of course not; all human emotions have their place. Sometimes, for example, some people need to feel angry in order to create enough leverage on themselves to make a change. However, we don't want to access our most negative and intense states as our first course of action, or when they're unwarranted, unnecessary, or inappropriate. **The goal is simply to consistently feel less pain and more pleasure in our lives.**

169

Transformational Vocabulary not only helps us eliminate patterns of pain, but can also increase our pleasure. **Start intensifying your experience of positive emotions by doing this exercise:**

1) Write down three words or phrases you regularly use to describe your positive states. Are they somewhat uninspiring?

2) Come up with three new words or phrases that will absolutely thrill you.

3) Enlist the aid of three of your friends in holding you to your new, higher standard. (For example, "Are you interested, or are you *absolutely unstoppable?*" "Does that make you feel happy, or *exuberant and impassioned?*") If you get leverage on yourself in the next ten days, you can begin to use these new words effectively.

170

Not only do words have a powerful impact on our emotions, but particular sets of words—those we use as metaphors—have an extraordinarily explosive effect. For example, you might say, "I'm *angry* with John." Or you could use a metaphor: "John *stabbed* me in the *back.*" Which description is more intense? Without a doubt, the thought of being stabbed will affect you more deeply.

When you use a metaphor, you're not describing your actual experience, but how it's *like* something else. Often our metaphors are far more intense than the reality. What did John really do? He may have broken a promise, but there's a big difference between that and being stabbed in the back, isn't there?

What metaphors do you consistently use to describe painful or frustrating experiences?

171

***Learning is the process of creating* a relationship between something you already understand and something new.** One way to do this is to use a metaphor for comparison.

Regardless of spiritual beliefs, most agree that Jesus Christ was a remarkable teacher. How did he teach? He used metaphors. When he approached fishermen, he didn't say, "I want you to go out and recruit Christians." He said, "I want you to become *fishers of men*." Utilizing the metaphor of fishing (something they already understood) and relating it to a new idea (sharing Christianity), he instantly taught them the process. A metaphor can take you from the darkness of misunderstanding to the light of clarity in a moment.

Next time you're confused, ask, "What's that like? Can you give me a metaphor?"

172

Even if we're unaware of it, we constantly use metaphors to describe aspects of our lives. Metaphors shape our life's perspective. For example, if I asked you to describe for me, "What is life? Give me a metaphor. What's it like?" you might describe life as a battle, and someone else might call it a game, or a test, or a dance. **These are called global metaphors because they affect many areas of your life simultaneously.**

If you approach everything from the viewpoint that life is a battle, what is life like? It's hard; you could lose or get killed; the next person you meet on the street could be your enemy. What if life is a game? It could actually be fun. What if life is a dance? Maybe there's a natural rhythm to it.

173

Which metaphor is the "right" one for you to use? **Probably all metaphors are useful at different times.** Sometimes you need life to be a game so that your perspective becomes more playful. Sometimes you need to see it as a sacred journey so that you appreciate and revere the gifts you've been given, whether they're friends, family, or opportunities. Sometimes it's useful to think of life as just a test or a challenge, especially when you find yourself facing a situation that seems to be without positive meaning. If you choose a different way to represent life, you'll automatically think, feel, and respond to situations in a brand new way.

How many other positive metaphors could you use to describe what life really means to you? Make a list now.

174

What would happen to your stress level if you consistently thought about dealing with various challenges in terms of "climbing the ladder of success" rather than "struggling to keep my head above water"? Would you feel different about taking a test if you talked about "sailing" through it rather than "flailing"? Would your perception of time change if you talked about it "flying" rather than "crawling"? You bet it would!

What metaphors do you use to describe the things you do every day? How do they make you feel? What new metaphors could you use to be more effective and make life more enjoyable?

175

Metaphors can provide hope. When things look bleak people often think, "This is going to go on forever." Instead, turn to a metaphor you have certainty about, e.g., "Life has its seasons, and I'm just in winter right now." Remember, some people freeze in the winter; others ski! Plus, what always follows winter? Spring!—just as the day follows night. The sun comes out, and you can plant new seeds. Then comes summer, and finally fall, when you get to reap your rewards.

Sometimes things don't work out exactly as planned—but **if you trust in the cycle of the seasons, you know that in the long term you will reap the harvest you have sown.**

176

If you feel that something is "holding you back" or that there's a "wall" blocking your progress, *look at the metaphors you're using.* Often you'll find you're using one that stops you from tapping the resources you have for solutions. It's hard to deal with a wall or something "invisible" that's holding you back.

Since you're the one who chose this metaphor in the first place, you can just as easily *change* it. If you feel like you've been "hitting the wall," why not stop hitting it and drill a hole through it? or climb over it? or tunnel under it? or just open the door and walk through it? or see it as a stepping-stone? **Changing your metaphor will change the way you deal with virtually anything.**

177

To remind yourself of the power of persistence, consider the metaphor of the stone cutter. How does he break open a giant boulder? He whacks it as hard as he can. The first hit doesn't leave even a scratch, but again he strikes—hundreds, maybe thousands of times.

He persists even when his actions seem to be futile. But he knows that **just because you don't see immediate results, it doesn't mean you're not making progress.** So he keeps striking the rock. At some point it doesn't just chip, but literally splits in two. Did the final blow break the boulder open? Of course not. It was the constant pressure being applied to the challenge at hand.

How can you apply this metaphor to your life in order to passionately persist?

178

Changing one global metaphor can instantly transform the way you look at your entire life. In one of my seminars there was a woman who found fault with everything—the room was too hot, then too cold; the person sitting in front of her was too tall. **Many people saw her as a "pain," but knowing that all behavior is belief-driven, I searched for the belief or metaphor that caused her to drive everyone else crazy.** Finally I uncovered it: "Small leaks sink the ship." If you thought anything that wasn't working could cause your ship to go down, wouldn't you be a little fanatical?

With a new global metaphor, she made a complete turnaround and became the class clown.

Which of your global metaphors could sink your ship?

179

Often the metaphors we use in one context, such as work, are **inappropriate for another context, such as our relationships.** One man I knew was so emotionally detached that his family didn't feel any connection with him at all. He never expressed his true feelings and always seemed to be directing them. Guess what he did for a living—he was an air traffic controller! The very essence of his job was to remain perfectly calm and detached, even in an emergency, so as not to alarm the pilots he was directing. While that attitude was necessary in the control tower, it didn't work at home.

Do any of your metaphors need to be replaced with ones more compatible with your situation? Could you help a friend with this knowledge?

180

Discover and take control of your metaphors with the following exercise:

1) Write down a few of the metaphors you have for life. Review your list and ask, "If life is like this, how would I feel about it?" What advantages and disadvantages are created by this metaphor?

2) List all the metaphors you link to one or two important areas of your life, such as your relationships or business. Are these metaphors empowering or disempowering? Just being aware of them can help you change them.

3) Create new, more empowering metaphors for life and for each of the areas you focused on.

4) Decide you are going to live with these new metaphors for the next 30 days, e.g., consistently remind yourself that this is what business is like...

181

Sometimes a metaphor is the best way **to help someone.**

When my son Josh was six years old, one of his friends died, and he came home in tears.

"Honey," I said, "I know how you feel. But that's because you're still a caterpillar." This broke his pattern. I then explained how, when a caterpillar encases itself in its cocoon, it looks as if it is dying. "But what's really happening?" I asked Josh.

"It's turning into a butterfly," he said.

"That's right," I said. "It's the beginning of a whole new life. You don't see your friend because he's really just flying above you, more beautiful and powerful than ever before. Sometimes we just have to trust that God knows when it's time for us to become butterflies..."

HOW TO USE YOUR ACTION SIGNALS

EMOTIONS

●

"There can be no transforming of darkness into light and of apathy into movement without emotion."

—CARL JUNG

182

You are the source of all your emotions. At any moment you can create or change them.

So why don't we? For most of us, feeling bad is "natural," yet we have to have a *reason* to feel good. **But you don't need an excuse to allow yourself to feel good.** You can just decide to feel good *right now,* simply because you're alive, simply because you want to. You don't have to wait for anything or anyone!

183

What's the best way to deal with negative emotions? There are several common, ineffective responses. You can *ignore* your emotions; of course they don't go away. You can *suppress* them, but they just come out in some other way. You can *indulge* in them and just feel sorry for yourself, but that doesn't make anything better. You can try to *compete* by saying, "You think you've got it bad? I've got it even worse!"

Of course, the more intelligent thing is to *transform* them by dealing effectively with the situation, looking for solutions, and *learning* from and *using* your emotions to enhance your life and the lives of all those you have the privilege to touch.

184

Understand that all emotions serve you. **Those you once thought of as negative emotions are merely *calls to action*.** For example, if you feel frustrated (and we'll explore this in more detail later) it means that you believe things could be better, and they're not. This is a call to action telling you there's something you must do to make this better now. This "negative" emotion is actually a gift if you use it effectively.

From now on, when you think of what you used to call a negative emotion, think of it as a call to action: an "action signal."

185

If you ever feel pain in any situation in your life, it's either the result of the way you're looking at things—your *perception* (focus)—or the result of what you're doing (your current approach, current actions). We might call this your *procedures.*

If you don't like the way you're feeling, **either change your focus or perception, or simply change what you're doing—your procedures—and you'll find an immediate difference in your emotions.** Find new ways to interact with your spouse or communicate with your boss—or change your perception that they must all agree with your point of view.

186

Whenever you feel a painful emotion, there are five steps you can take very quickly to *learn from* and *use* this action signal:

1) Identify what you're *really* feeling.

2) Acknowledge and appreciate your emotions. Know that at some level they are supporting you to make a positive change by calling you to action.

3) Get curious! Realize that this emotion is offering you a message to change something. Do you need to change your perception or your procedures?

4) Get confident that you can handle this emotion immediately because you have done so in the past. Remember a time when you successfully handled this emotion and model what you did to learn what to do today and in the future.

5) Get excited, and take action!

187

Getting "curious" about your emotions can be tough when you're in the heat of the moment. *Here are four questions to ask yourself to get on the path to learning from and using your action signals:*

1) How do I really want to feel right now?
2) What would I have to believe in order to feel the way I've been feeling?
3) What am I willing to do to create a solution and handle this right now?
4) What can I learn from this?

188

To gain confidence about your ability to handle a negative emotion, remember a time when you felt a similar way: **Realize that you've successfully handled this emotion before.** Do you remember a time when you felt depressed and turned it around? Or were you frustrated or overwhelmed, yet you refocused and felt centered?

Model your own successful actions from the past. What did you do then that worked? Did you change what you were focusing on? Did you ask yourself a better question? Did you interrupt your pattern by changing physiology, going for a walk, returning in a more balanced state?

If you begin to feel this emotion again, use the same strategies you used in the past to turn it around.

189

Mentally rehearse handling potentially difficult situations in which negative emotions might be triggered in the future. **See, hear, and feel yourself handling the situation easily** until you've conditioned yourself with a sense of certainty that you can confidently and powerfully deal with anything that occurs.

190

My philosophy is to "kill the monster while it's little." **The best time to handle a "negative" emotion is when you first begin to feel it.** It's much more difficult to interrupt an emotional pattern once it's full-blown.

ACTION SIGNAL #1

Uncomfortable emotions like boredom, impatience, unease, distress, or mild embarrassment are sending you a nagging message that something is not quite right. ***Either your perception of the situation is making you uncomfortable, or your current actions are not supporting you in your goal.***

The Solution

1) Use the skills you learned in Section 2 of this book to immediately change your emotional state.

2) Clarify how you want to feel now or what you want to accomplish.

3) Change or refine your actions. Try a slightly different approach to see if you can immediately change the way you're feeling about the situation or if you can change the results you're producing. Like all emotions that aren't dealt with, Action Signal #1 will grow into something more intense, possibly Action Signal #2.

192

ACTION SIGNAL #2

If we don't deal with situations that are making us uncomfortable, often they grow into fear. The emotions of *fear,* apprehension, worry, and anxiety are simply a call to action telling you that **you need to be more prepared for what's about to occur.**

The Solution

1) Think about the situation you're feeling fearful about and decide what you must do right now to prepare yourself mentally or physically.

2) Figure out what actions you need to take to deal with the situation in the most effective way possible.

3) Once you've prepared yourself, decide to stop worrying, then visualize yourself consistently and successfully dealing with this situation until you feel a sense of continued confidence.

ACTION SIGNAL #3

The action signal of hurt *comes from a feeling of loss.* The sense of loss is often illusory.

This action signal is calling us to **change our perception or realize that our expectations may have been inappropriate.**

The Solution

1) Realize you may not have actually "lost" anything. Raised voices do not necessarily mean someone no longer loves you.
2) Reevaluate the situation by asking: Is it possible that by not having my expectations met, I've actually *gained* something else? Have I judged this situation too soon or too harshly?
3) As elegantly and appropriately as possible, communicate your feeling to whoever you see as its source: "I know you really care about me. Can you clarify for me what really happened?"

194

ACTION SIGNAL #4

The action signal of anger, *annoyance, resentment, or rage* is a powerful emotion. Its source is feelings of hurt that have not been dealt with.

This action signal tells us that **one of our important standards, or rules, has been violated by ourselves or someone else.**

The Solution

1) Realize you may have misinterpreted, and the person you believe has "broken your rules" may not even know they've broken them.

2) Realize that your rules are not necessarily the "right" rules (sometimes that's hard to do).

3) Interrupt the anger by asking yourself such questions as "In the long run, is it true that this person really cares about me? What can I learn from this? How can I communicate the importance of my standards?"

195

ACTION SIGNAL #5

The action signal of frustration means that in spite of your current lack of progress, at some level you believe that something you're doing could be done better, that you could be getting a greater result. This is a call to action telling you to **change your approach and you can still achieve what you want.**

The Solution

1) Be flexible! Realize that frustration is your friend, and brainstorm new ways to get a result.

2) Find a role model, someone who has found a way to get what you want, and learn from him or her.

3) Become fascinated by what you could learn to help you handle this challenge in a way that consumes very little time or energy and actually creates joy.

196

ACTION SIGNAL #6

The action signal of disappointment is the painful feeling of being let down based on the belief that you're going to miss out on something forever. This action signal calls you to **change your expectations.**

The Solution

1) Figure out what you can learn from this situation, or change your expectations.

2) Set a new, even more inspiring goal toward which you can make immediate progress.

3) Realize that you may be judging too soon. Often the things you're disappointed about are only temporary challenges.

4) Have patience. Reevaluate what you truly want, and begin to develop an even more effective plan for achieving it.

5) Cultivate an attitude of positive expectancy about what will happen in the future, regardless of what has occurred in the past.

197

ACTION SIGNAL #7

The action signal of <u>guilt</u> tells you that you have violated one of your own highest standards, and that **you must do something immediately to ensure that you correct the situation and keep yourself from ever violating it again.** This is how we maintain internal integrity.

The Solution

1) Acknowledge that you've violated your own critical standards.

2) Absolutely commit to making sure you'll never repeat this behavior. Mentally and emotionally rehearse how you'd deal with the same situation again in a way consistent with your highest personal standards.

3) Don't wallow in guilt. Now that you've utilized it to get yourself back in line, let go of it—do the right thing! Continually beating yourself up will not help you or anyone else to be better.

ACTION SIGNAL #8

The action signal of inadequacy is telling you that **you don't believe you currently have the information, understanding, strategies, or confidence you need for the task at hand.** It's a call to gather additional resources.

The Solution

1) Maybe you've applied completely unfair criteria for assessing your performance. Ask yourself, "Is it possible I really do have the ability to deal with this, and it's only my perception making me feel inadequate?"

2) If you decide that you really don't have the skills to deal with the situation, appreciate your feelings of inadequacy as a call to improve yourself.

3) Find a role model who's effective in this area and learn some simple things you can do immediately to become more adequate or effective in this area.

199

ACTION SIGNAL #9

The action signals of <u>overload, overwhelm,</u> grief, depression, and helplessness occur when we think of all the things that have happened to us that we cannot control.

You must break the situation down into simple steps.

The Solution

1) Decide which of the many things you're dealing with are absolutely essential to focus on.

2) Prioritize the most important steps for making progress in this area, thus gaining a sense of control.

3) Immediately tackle the first simple item on your list.

4) In dealing with all-encompassing emotions like grief, focus on what you *can* control. Realize that there must be some empowering meaning to it all. Remember, everything in life happens for a reason and a purpose, and it will serve you.

200

ACTION SIGNAL #10

The action signal of <u>loneliness</u> tells you that you need a connection with people, that you really care about them and love being with them. It's calling you to **reach out and connect.**

The Solution

1) Realize that you can reach out and make a connection *immediately.* Caring people are everywhere.

2) Identify what kind of connection you need: basic friendship? love? a sympathetic ear?

3) Take immediate action to reach out and connect with someone.

201

How can you ensure that you always have the Action Signals in front of you to help you break unresourceful patterns? Write them all down on a 3" × 5" card you can carry everywhere. When an upsetting situation occurs, focus on the meaning the emotion really has for you and what action you can take to utilize it. Attach one of these little cards to the sun visor in your car so you can review it throughout the day—especially if you get stuck in traffic!

Next, we'll learn the ten Emotions of Power you can use immediately to replace any negative pattern.

202

EMOTION OF POWER #1

Cultivate the emotions of love and warmth. A marvelous core belief to adopt comes from *A Course in Miracles:* **All communication is either a loving response or a cry for help.** If someone comes to you in a state of hurt or anger, and you consistently respond with love and warmth, eventually that person's state will change and his or her intensity will melt away.

203

EMOTION OF POWER #2

Cultivate the emotions of <u>appreciation</u> and <u>gratitude</u>. These are among the most spiritual emotions we can have, and they enhance our lives more than almost anything I know. **Live with an attitude of gratitude!**

204

EMOTION OF POWER #3

Cultivate curiosity. If you really want to grow in your lifetime, learn to be as inquisitive as a child. Curious people are never bored, and for them, **life becomes an unending study of joy.**

205

EMOTION OF POWER #4

Cultivate the feelings of <u>excitement</u> and <u>passion</u>. These can turn any challenge into a tremendous opportunity, giving us the unbridled power to move our lives forward at a faster tempo than ever before. **Ignite your passion** by using your physiology: Speak more rapidly, visualize images more quickly, and move your body in the direction you want to go.

206

EMOTION OF POWER #5

Determination makes the difference between being stuck and being struck with the **lightning power of commitment!** Merely "pushing" yourself won't do it; putting yourself in a state of determination will.

207

EMOTION OF POWER #6

Adopt an attitude of flexibility. If there's one emotion to cultivate to guarantee success, it's the ability to change your approach. In fact, **all the action signals are just messages to be more flexible!** Throughout your life there will be situations you won't be able to control. Your ability to be flexible in your rules, the meaning you attach to things, and your actions will determine your long-term success or failure, not to mention your level of personal joy.

208

EMOTION OF POWER #7

Consistently experience confidence. If you've ever done anything successfully, you can do it again. Plus, through the power of faith, you can be confident even in environments and situations you've never previously encountered. **Imagine and feel certain now about the emotions you deserve to have** instead of waiting for them to spontaneously appear someday in the far distant future.

209

EMOTION OF POWER #8

Cheerfulness enhances your self-esteem, makes life more fun, and causes the people around you to feel happier as well. Being cheerful does not mean that you're Pollyanna or that you look at the world through rose-colored glasses and refuse to acknowledge challenges. It means **you're incredibly intelligent because you know that if you live in a state of pleasure and positive anticipation—one that's so intense that you transmit a sense of joy to those around you —you can have the impact to meet any challenge that comes your way.**

210

EMOTION OF POWER #9

Nurturing your own vitality is critical; if you don't take care of your health, it's more difficult to be able to enjoy your emotions. Contrary to popular belief, sitting still doesn't preserve energy. The human nervous system needs to *move* to have energy. As you move, oxygen flows through your system, and **that physical level of health creates the emotional sense of vitality you need in order to turn challenges into opportunities.**

211

EMOTION OF POWER #10

There's no richer emotion I know than the sense of contribution: feeling that who you are as a person, how you've lived your life, what you've said and done, has touched others in a deep and meaningful manner is the ultimate gift in life. ***The secret to living is giving.***

212

For the next two days, anytime you feel a disempowering emotion, remember to listen to the messages of this action signal. *Use the ten Emotions of Power as antidotes as you utilize the solution that is inherent in every "negative" emotion.*

TAKE THE TEN-DAY MENTAL CHALLENGE

MENTAL CHALLENGE AND MASTER SYSTEM OF EVALUATION

●

"Man's mind stretched to a new idea never goes back to its original dimensions."

—OLIVER WENDELL HOLMES

213

The mark of a true champion is consistency. After all, who wants to create results just once in a while? Who wants to feel joyous for only a moment or be at peak performance only sporadically? We want to *consistently* experience all of the emotions that make life worthwhile.

So how do you establish consistency? It's all based on your habits. **Knowing what to do is not enough; you must do what you know.**

214

The same kind of thinking that has brought us to where we are will not get us where we want to go. Change is our greatest ally, yet so many—whether individuals, corporations, or communities—resist it, justifying their current strategies by pointing to the success they now enjoy. Yet an entirely different approach may be required in order to produce a new level of personal and professional success.

215

Would you buy a new Ferrari only to let it sit in your driveway? Would you purchase the most up-to-date computer only to pack it away in the closet?

I'm sure your answer would be a resounding "No!" By the same token, would you read this book and fail to use the powerful tools it contains? I suspect not. That's why, throughout this section, I'll offer you a simple plan for interrupting your old patterns of thinking, feeling, and behaving, and show you how to immediately put into practice some of the new, empowering strategies you've already learned. **I guarantee that if you follow this plan to the letter, you'll be able to make your new emotional patterns absolutely consistent!**

216

Yes, it's true: We can't control the wind or the rain or the other vagaries of weather. But we can tack our sails such that we can steer the course we desire.

217

Every successful person I know has the capacity to remain centered, clear, and powerful in the midst of emotional "storms." How is this accomplished? I've discovered that most of these individuals have a fundamental rule: **Never spend more than 10 percent of your time on the problem, and always spend at least 90 percent of your time on the solution.**

218

How can you take immediate control of your mental and emotional patterns? You're about to discover one of the most effective strategies ever devised, a blend of realism and optimism. Years ago, thinking positively was not high on my list of solutions. I thought I was being smart by refusing to see things as better than they were.

In truth, life is a balance. If we refuse to see the weeds taking root in our gardens, our delusions will destroy us. Equally destructive, however, is to misperceive the garden as overrun. The path of leaders is one of balance.

1) **See the situation as it is** (don't see it as worse than it is).
2) **See it better than it is.**
3) **Make it the way you see it!**

219

The single most important step in weeding the gardens of our minds is to interrupt our limiting patterns. And the best way to accomplish this is to take the Ten-Day Mental Challenge, thereby taking conscious control of our thoughts. **This process is a splendid opportunity to eliminate negative and destructive patterns.**

Quite simply, the challenge is this: *For the next ten days, beginning immediately, commit to taking full control of all your mental and emotional faculties.* Decide right now that you will not indulge in or dwell on any unresourceful thoughts or emotions for *ten consecutive days.*

220

THE TEN-DAY MENTAL CHALLENGE

Welcome to ten days unlike any you've lived before! Here are the rules of the game:

1) For the next ten *consecutive* days, refuse to dwell on any unresourceful thoughts or feelings. Refuse to indulge in any disempowering questions or devitalizing vocabulary or metaphors.

2) When you catch yourself beginning to focus on the negative, use any of the techniques you've learned to redirect your focus immediately, starting with the Problem-Solving Questions as your first line of attack.

3) Set yourself up for success each morning for the next ten days by asking yourself the Morning Power Questions.

221

THE TEN-DAY MENTAL CHALLENGE (Continued)

4) For the next ten *consecutive* days, make certain that your entire focus is on solutions and not on problems. The moment you perceive a possible challenge, immediately focus on a possible solution.

5) If you catch yourself indulging in an unresourceful thought or feeling, don't beat yourself up—as long as you change your state immediately. However, *if you continue to dwell on unresourceful thoughts or feelings for any measurable length of time,* you must wait until the following morning, *then start the ten days over again,* regardless of how many days in a row you've already completed.

222

Are you really ready to take a fresh approach to life? Don't begin this ten-day commitment unless and until you are certain you are going to live by it for the entire length of time. **This is not a challenge for the weak at heart.** It's only for those who are truly dedicated to conditioning their nervous systems for new, empowering emotional patterns that can take them to higher levels of success. It's for those who want to make everything they've learned intellectually—NAC, questions, Transformational Vocabulary, metaphors, changing focus and physiology—a part of their daily experience.

223

How can you gain additional leverage to ensure that you stick to the Ten-Day Mental Challenge? **Announce to your friends, family, and associates what you're doing, and enlist their support in helping you stay on track.** Or, even better, find a partner who wants to take the Ten-Day Mental Challenge with you.

It's also an excellent idea to keep a written journal the whole time you're meeting the Mental Challenge. By recording how you successfully deal with unresourceful patterns, you'll be creating an invaluable road map you can review in the future whenever you seem to hit a detour.

224

Years ago I got hooked on a habit that has turned out to be one of the most valuable of my life: reading at least 30 minutes a day. Jim Rohn, one of my teachers, told me that reading something of substance, something of value, something that was nourishing, something that taught you new distinctions, was more important than eating. "Miss a meal," he said, "but don't miss your reading."

So while you're taking the Ten-Day Mental Challenge and cleansing your system, nourish it with reading material that yields insights and strategies to guide you in the new lifestyle you've chosen. Remember: **leaders are readers.**

225

What will the Ten-Day Mental Challenge do for you?

1) It will make you acutely aware of all the habitual mental patterns that hold you back.

2) It will force you to search for empowering alternatives.

3) It will give you an incredible jolt of confidence every time you take control of your thought processes to turn your situation around.

4) Most important, it will help you to create new habits, new standards, and new expectations that will lead you to a richer experience of life.

   Success is processional; it results from a series of small disciplines. Like a freight train picking up speed, this exercise in leaving behind old patterns and fueling yourself with new ones will give you unprecedented momentum.

226

Is this just a ten-day exercise? Not really. **You never have to return to your old negative patterns again if you don't want to.** This is your opportunity to become "addicted" to a positive focus for the rest of your life.

If after banishing your toxic mental patterns for ten days, you wish to return, be my guest. But I'm willing to bet that once you've become aware of the possibilities, going back would seem disgusting. Just remember that if you ever get off track, you know how to use a variety of tools to put yourself back on the high road—immediately.

227

One of the things I love most is the opportunity to unravel the mystery of human behavior and offer solutions that truly enhance the quality of people's lives. Probing beneath the surface, I locate key leverage points —global beliefs, metaphors, etc.—for facilitating change. Every day I live the role of Sherlock Holmes, piecing together the jigsaw puzzle of each person's unique background.

While there are telltale clues to human behavior just as blatant as the smoking gun, sometimes the clues are a little more subtle and take further investigation to uncover. Ultimately, however, it all comes down to specific key elements. The difference in people is how they reason. **The way they decide what things mean and what they should do I call the Master System of Evaluation.**

228

The importance of understanding human behavior is best shown with a metaphor. Imagine someone standing on a riverbank. Suddenly he hears a cry for help and sees a man drowning, so he leaps in and rescues him. As he's catching his breath, he hears more screams and again jumps into the river, this time rescuing two people. Before he even has a chance to recover, he hears four more people calling for help.

The rest of his day is spent pulling person after person from the raging waters. If only he had walked a short distance upriver, he could have discovered who was throwing all those people in the water in the first place!

What efforts could you save yourself by addressing problems at their *cause* instead of their *effect?*

229

Once you understand the Master System of Evaluation, you are better equipped to influence your own behavior and that of others. There is a clear science to the way you evaluate your life's problems and opportunities. **Understanding the components of your decision-making system can help you not only understand your own behavior, but anticipate what you'll be repelled from and pulled toward.** As you'll soon see, there are five components that determine how you evaluate anything—from what you should have for dinner to whether or not you should be married.

Each one of us has a unique combination of these components, and this is what causes our lives to be equally unique.

230

In dealing with upsets in a relationship, wouldn't it be great to understand people's behavior so you can reconnect with them immediately? In a marriage, it's especially important to see through the day-to-day stresses so you can nurture the bond that first brought you together. If your spouse is feeling pressure from work and vents frustration, it doesn't mean that your marriage is over. It does indicate that you need to be more attentive and to focus on supporting this person you love. You wouldn't judge the stock market solely on one day when it plunged 30 points; by the same token, you can't judge a person's character on one isolated incident. **People are not their behaviors.** Understand what drives them, and you will really know them.

231

If there's one thing I've learned **in seeking out the core beliefs and strategies of today's leaders, it's that superior evaluations create a superior life.** For example, those who succeed financially have better ways of evaluating opportunities' risks and rewards. Although everyone has access to pretty much the same information, it's financial masters' system for deciding what things mean and what they should do that gives them the edge. Those who have lasting relationships are superior in evaluating how to respond to their spouse in stressful situations. Those who are happier have a more effective way of evaluating life's "problems." The good news is that you can save yourself years of pain by modeling the strategies of those who are already succeeding.

232

Unless we take control of our evaluation procedures, they can lead us down a path that makes us question our abilities. Imagine playing tennis and hitting a poor serve. More often than not, people start generalizing in a disempowering way: "What a terrible serve!" becomes "I couldn't play today to save my life." Don't get caught in this self-defeating cycle!

Right now, identify at least one incident you may have exaggerated negatively. Have you done this with your relationships? your job performance? your physical abilities? Decide now to interrupt this pattern. Shout "Erase!" next time you begin it. Let go and focus on what you want to achieve. Notice the immediate change this produces.

233

A common denominator among successful people is that they consistently make superior evaluations. Hockey great Wayne Gretzky is no exception. Is he the biggest, strongest, or fastest player in the league? By his own admission, the answer is no.

When I asked him what makes him so effective, he said that **while most players skate to where the puck is, he skates *where the puck is going*.** His ability to anticipate—to evaluate the velocity and direction of the puck, the strategies and momentum of the other players —allows him to place himself in the best position for scoring.

If you were to apply a little bit of foresight to a situation you're in right now, can you see how that might make a huge difference?

234

Have there been times when someone has said something to you that made you cry, while the same comment another time might have made you laugh? Very likely the difference could be traced to the state you were in. Your mental/emotional state is the first element of your Master System of Evaluation.

If you're in a state of confidence and positive expectancy, the decisions you make will be quite different than if you're feeling vulnerable and fearful. While it makes sense to be cautious in some situations, this can hamper you at other times. Make certain that when you're deciding what events mean and what to do, you're in an extremely resourceful state rather than in a reactive survival mode.

235

Questions form the second building block of your Master System. Before you do anything, you must evaluate: "What does this mean, and what must I do to avoid pain and/or gain pleasure?"

Whether or not you take action is strongly influenced by the specific questions you ask yourself. If you're considering making a date with someone, do you habitually agonize, "What if this person rejects me or is offended when I approach?" If so, then you're likely to lead yourself through a series of evaluations causing you to pass up the opportunity. If, however, you ask such questions as "Won't it be great to get to know this person? How much more fun will I have by connecting with this person?" these questions will surely cause you to seize the moment!

236

We all want to feel more pleasure and less pain, but we've each learned different lessons about what will lead to these. **As a result, each of us has learned to *value* certain emotions more highly than others.** For example, some people's idea of ultimate pleasure is security, while others' is adventure. Your hierarchy of values, the third element of the Master System, is merely a list of the states you believe are most important for you to experience (pleasure-producing) and most important to avoid (pain-producing). All your decisions are driven by your unconscious desire to achieve your pleasure values and avoid your pain values. For example, if you value love but want to avoid conflict at all costs, would this affect your level of honesty in a personal relationship?

237

The fourth element of your Master System is your beliefs. Global beliefs determine your expectations for yourself, other people, and life in general; often they control what you're even willing to evaluate in the first place. One special category of beliefs is rules; they tell you what must happen in order to feel that your values have been met. For example, some people believe, "If you love me, then you'll never raise your voice." This rule will cause the person to evaluate a raised voice as evidence that there is no love in the relationship, even though this may have no basis in fact.

Can you think of a rule or other belief you have for relationships? Has it helped or hindered you?

238

How do we build beliefs? The fifth element in your Master System is your *references*—the hodgepodge of experiences and information stored in the giant filing cabinet called your brain. This is the raw material you use to construct the beliefs that guide your decisions. **You have unlimited experiences (references) to call upon;** which ones you choose will determine the meaning you pull from an experience, how you feel about it, and what you'll do.

As one example of the importance of references, can you see how it would make a difference if you grew up feeling you were consistently being taken advantage of, as opposed to growing up feeling unconditionally loved? disciplined vs. indulged? How might this affect the way you learned to evaluate life, people, or opportunity?

239

To stimulate your thinking about how the Master System works, *let me ask you a question: What is your most treasured memory?*

In answering it, what did you do? Probably your first step was to repeat the *question.* Then you probably searched your *references,* reviewing the myriad experiences of your life before selecting one.

But maybe you refused to pick one because you have a *belief* that all life's experiences are treasured or that selecting one would denigrate the rest. Perhaps you had difficulty even recalling any memories, treasured or otherwise, because the feelings you associate with "living in the past" are *values* you avoid.

Do you see how your Master System determines not only what and how you evaluate, but even what you're willing to evaluate?

240

What creates mastery? Invariably, masters are simply those who have more references than the rest of us about what leads to success or frustration in a given area. Each day presents another opportunity to take in new references that can help us bolster our beliefs, refine our values, ask new questions, and access the states that propel us in the direction we desire.

241

You can immediately make global changes that simultaneously affect how you think, feel, and act in multiple areas of your life. How? Simply by shifting any one of the five elements of your Master System.

For example, rather than just conditioning yourself to feel differently about rejection, you could adopt a new global *belief* such as "I am the source of all my emotions. Nothing and no one can change how I feel except me. If I find myself in reaction to anything, I can change it in a moment." If you were to fervently embrace this belief, could you see how it would eliminate not only your fear of rejection, but also your feelings of anger or frustration or inadequacy? Suddenly, **you become the master of your fate.**

242

Another way to instantly overcome feelings of rejection or inadequacy is to change your *values* hierarchy, ranking contribution or gratitude, for example, at the top. Then, if someone rejected you, it wouldn't matter: rather than focus on your perceived shortcomings, you'd concentrate on what you could still contribute in order to help the person or improve the situation in some way. Or you'd feel so grateful for your life that no amount of rejection could affect you. In fact, you wouldn't even perceive it as such. These emotions would cause you to feel permeated with an unprecedented sense of joy and connection.

Simply by shifting *any* of the five elements of your Master System of Evaluation, you can instantly transform every area of your life.

243

Have you ever had difficulty keeping a simple commitment such as going to the gym? Most likely you've been making it too complex, focusing on the *dozens* of individual things you must do. You might think, "It's just too much trouble to work out." You have to drive to the facility, park your car, check in, find a locker, change your clothes, work out, shower, etc.

Yet when you think of things that are easy to do, you "chunk" them very differently. Want to eat? You bet! Want to go to the beach? In a heartbeat! What has to be done? Just hop in your car and do it!

The difference is not the tasks, merely how you evaluate them. Change your evaluations, and you immediately change your life.

YOUR PERSONAL COMPASS

VALUES AND RULES

•

*"Nothing splendid has ever been achieved
except by those who dared believe that something
inside of them was superior to circumstance."*

—BRUCE BARTON

244

If we want the deepest fulfillment, we can achieve it only one way: by deciding what we desire most in life—what our highest *values* are—then committing to live by our decision every single day.

245

Who are the most universally admired people in our culture? Aren't they those who have a solid grasp of their own values, people who not only profess their standards, but *live* by them? **We all respect men and women who take a stand for what they believe, even if we don't agree with their ideas about what's right or wrong.** There is undeniable strength in individuals who congruently lead lives in which their philosophies and actions are one.

Make congruency your goal: Is there anything you currently do that's inconsistent with what you believe is right? Take immediate action to rectify this. Then think for a moment: What's a value or a principle you absolutely live by, and how has it enhanced your life?

246

In the movie Stand and Deliver, *teacher Jaime Escalante* forcefully demonstrates **the power wielded by those who have absolute clarity about what they value most, what they stand for.** His passion for learning was transmitted to his students not by a teaching technique but by his living demonstration of what was possible. He taught a generation considered "lost" not only how to pass a calculus test (something they were certain couldn't be done), but also how to value one another, their Latino heritage, and the power of learning to raise the quality of their lives forever. His absolute commitment to a higher set of standards transformed these young people's lives.

What could you accomplish if you were absolutely focused on what you value most in life?

247

If love, success, or integrity are important to you, then they are part of your values system. **A *value* is an emotional state** you feel is very important either to experience (because of the pleasure you believe it will bring) or to avoid (because of the pain you associate to it).

All our decision making is driven by these beliefs: How will a given action help us move toward a pleasure value? Will it help us avoid or move away from a pain value?

What's one of the most important pleasurable emotions you value, and what's a painful emotion you'll do almost anything to avoid?

248

Pleasure values are known as moving-toward values; they include such emotions as love, joy, freedom, security, passion, and peace of mind.

Pain values (e.g., rejection, depression, loneliness) are known as *moving-away-from values.* **As we make decisions we consider whether these pain or pleasure states will be a consequence of our actions.**

In the next few days you'll begin to clarify not only the emotional states that drive all your decisions, but also their order of importance. For example, you may value both security and adventure. Determining which one is more important to you will help you be much more effective in making decisions consistent with what will give you long-term happiness.

249

In addition to "moving-toward" and "moving-away-from" values, there are two other categories of values: *end values* and *means values*.

For example, you may say you value your car, but it's merely a means to an end. In contrast, **the *end value* you seek is an emotional state,** such as excitement (Pontiac), prestige (Mercedes), or safety (Volvo).

Remember, our desire to meet our end values is the driving force behind all decision making. Unfortunately, people often make decisions out of their desire to meet their means values (goals) yet fail to achieve what's most important: their end values (their lives' driving emotional needs).

250

Have you ever said, "I really want to be in a relationship"? Then you finally found one, and after a short time you realized, "I don't want a relationship!"? The reason is that the relationship was only a means to an end. What you really wanted was what you *thought* a relationship would give you: the end values of love, companionship, or intimacy. Relationships don't automatically lead to these more important values. You must know that these are your *real goals*, and consistently interact with them in mind.

Remember, you can achieve your means values in life (money, position, degree, children, relationships) and still be unhappy. **Unless you live consistent with your deepest (end) values, you'll achieve but still lack the ultimate fulfillment you truly deserve.**

251

Although there are many emotional states we consider personal values, we hold some more dear than others. Again, those we'll do the most to attain can be called our *moving-toward* values, such as love, success, freedom, intimacy, security, adventure, power, passion, comfort, and health.

Once you've identified your values, you can delve further to uncover a *hierarchy* into which they fit. Of the examples just listed, which would you deem more important than others?

Take a moment now to rank them from 1 to 10, 1 being the emotional state you regard most highly.

VALUE	RANKING	VALUE	RANKING
Love		Adventure	
Success		Power	
Freedom		Passion	
Intimacy		Comfort	
Security		Health	

252

Just as with moving-toward values, **we each have a hierarchy of states that we'll do the most to avoid.** Some of the more common *moving-away-from* values are rejection, anger, frustration, loneliness, depression, failure, humiliation, and guilt.

Rank these examples from 1 to 8, 1 being the emotional state you'd work the hardest to avoid having to feel.

VALUE	RANKING	VALUE	RANKING
Rejection		Depression	
Anger		Failure	
Frustration		Humiliation	
Loneliness		Guilt	

253

If I asked you to go skydiving, would you? It would depend, among other things, on the dynamics of your values hierarchy. For example, if your top moving-toward value was security, and your top moving-away-from value was fear (meaning you'd do almost anything to avoid it), you probably wouldn't go!

But what if your top moving-away-from value was *rejection,* and you thought your friends would turn on you if you didn't go? Since people will do more to avoid pain than to gain pleasure, your need to avoid rejection could win out over your attachment to the need to feel secure.

Have you ever felt pushed by one value while being pulled back by another? **Decision making is nothing but values clarification.**

254

One of the most important reasons to clarify your values hierarchy is to uncover any *values conflicts* that may be holding you back. For example, if *success* is your top moving-toward value, and *rejection* is your top moving-away-from value, do you see how these two impulses could work at cross-purposes? **Trying to achieve the pleasure of success without risking the pain of rejection would never work.** In fact, you'd probably sabotage your success before getting very far, because the fear of rejection would prevent you from taking the risks that are necessary to achieve any kind of meaningful success.

The solution, which is described in the next few pages of this book, is a two-step process of awareness and conscious decision making.

255

STEP #1A: VALUES AWARENESS

All you must do to discover your moving-toward values is to ask yourself one question: ***What's most important to me in life?*** Brainstorm your answers, keeping in mind that you want to discover your *end* values, the emotional states you most desire to feel.

After making your list, rank them in their order of importance; e.g., #1 is the state you value most, #2 is the next most highly valued, etc.

256

STEP #1B: VALUES AWARENESS

To discover your moving-away-from values, ask yourself, ***"What emotions are most important for me to avoid having to feel?** What feelings would I do almost anything to avoid?"* Brainstorm your answers.

After making your list, rank them in their order of importance; e.g., #1 is the state you'd do the most to avoid having to feel (it offers the most potential pain), #2 is the next most intense emotional state, etc.

257

STEP #2: MAKING CONSCIOUS DECISIONS

By eliciting your current values, you've discovered what priorities have been conditioned into your life and the system of pain and pleasure that's been driving you. **But if you want to take an active role in designing your life—starting over from the beginning, if need be —you must make some new decisions today.**

Ask yourself these questions:

1) What do my values *need to be* in order to create my ultimate destiny, in order for me to be the best person I could possibly be, in order for me to have the largest impact in my lifetime?

2) What other values do I *need to add* to my list of life priorities?

258

What have you accomplished by creating a new list of values? Isn't it just a bunch of words on a piece of paper? The answer is yes—if you don't *condition* yourself to use them as your new life compass. If you do, however, **your values will aid you in negotiating peaceful seas and raging storms, enabling you to steer the course you've charted toward your destiny.**

Keep them in front of you throughout the day. Give a copy of your list to friends as leverage to stay on track. Visualize, think, and feel the benefits of living by these values until your anticipation of the emotional rewards conditions you to make them a part of your everyday experience.

259

What has to happen in order for you to feel good? Do you have to be hugged, made love to, told how much you're respected? make a million dollars? play under-par golf? be acknowledged by your boss? drive the right car? go to the right parties? achieve spiritual enlightenment? or just appreciate a sunset?

The truth is that nothing has to happen in order for you to feel good. You can feel good *right now* if you choose to! After all, when all this happens, who's going to make you feel good? You are!

So why wait? The only thing that's stopping you is your *rule* (a belief) that all these things have to happen before you can feel good. Break these arbitrary rules, and experience the joy you deserve.

260

If you're going to have a rule for happiness, make it this: **"Nothing has to happen for me to feel good! I feel good because I'm alive! Life is a gift, and I revel in it."** Abraham Lincoln once said, "Most people are as happy as they decide to be." The story of his life and the stories of other people who have triumphed over tragedies are important reminders that we are in control.

Adopt this rule and decide to raise your standards for the one thing over which you have complete control—yourself. It means you've committed to being intelligent, flexible, and creative enough to consistently find a way to look at your life in a fashion that makes any experience enriching.

261

How do we know whether we're living in accordance with our values? It depends completely upon our *rules:* those beliefs we hold about what has to happen in order to feel successful, or happy, or healthy.

It's as if we have a miniature court system set up in our brains. **Our personal rules are the ultimate judge and jury,** deciding whether our actions have met the criteria necessary for us to celebrate the attainment of a certain value; they determine whether we feel good or bad about any situation, whether we give ourselves pain or pleasure.

262

An important question to answer whenever we consistently feel pain in our lives is, "Is this pain the result of my situation or of my rules for how I should feel about it? Is my feeling bad about this making it better? What rule (belief) must I have in order to feel bad in this situation?"

It's critical to examine our rules to make certain they're intelligent and appropriate. Some people's rules for feeling good are that their children must be getting straight A's in school, they must be #1 in their office in sales, have less than 10 percent body fat, and feel calm and unstressed at all times! Can you imagine how often someone with these rules would feel good?

Examine your rules. Make sure they serve you!

263

It's amazing how many people have created seemingly unlimited ways to feel bad (pain rules), and only a few ways to feel good (pleasure rules).

Right now, decide on a quality rule to adopt in order to allow yourself to feel loved more often. Rather than having your rule for love be "Only when a person constantly tells me they love me...buys me expensive gifts...takes me on exotic trips...touches me constantly... and is willing to do things they hate, just to make me happy"—which would clearly limit how often you'd feel loved—maybe you could simplify your rules to "I feel love anytime I think loving thoughts or express my love or warmth to anyone."

264

Are the rules that govern your life today still suitable for who you've become? **Have you hung on to rules that helped you in the past, but hurt you in the present?** For example, at one point in your life it may have been very important to be the toughest person around and to never show your emotions. However, while this rule may have helped you in the school yard, it may not be very effective for creating a lasting personal relationship.

Likewise, if your profession is one of a lawyer, be careful about carrying the metaphor of your work—and the rules that come with it—home. Otherwise you'll be cross-examining your spouse each evening.

What rules from your past can you let go of now?

265

How do you know you're successful? Two men with different rules for success attended one of my seminars. One was a prominent executive with every reason to feel on top of the world: a happy marriage, five beautiful children, a seven-figure income, and a body sculpted by marathon running. Yet he felt like a failure. Why? He had completely unreasonable rules.

By contrast, another man who had none of the executive's "advantages" felt truly successful. When I asked him what had to happen for him to feel successful, he answered, "All I have to do is wake up in the morning, look down, and see that I am above ground—because **every day above ground is a great day!"**

Which of these men do you think is more successful?

266

We certainly want to use the power of goals, the allure of a compelling future, to pull ourselves forward. **But we must make sure that underneath it all we have rules that allow us to be happy whenever we want.**

What has to happen for you to feel happy or successful? secure? loved?

267

How do you know if a rule disempowers you and needs to be changed? Your rule is disempowering if

1) It's impossible to meet (if your criteria are so complex or numerous or rigid that you can't ever win the game of life).

2) Something you can't control determines whether or not the rule is met (e.g., if other people have to respond to you in a certain way before you can be happy).

3) It gives you only a few ways to feel good and lots of ways to feel bad (e.g., if you feel good only when everything happens exactly as anticipated, vs. feeling bad when anything else occurs).

268

Right now, begin to **take control of your rules.** *Answer the following questions as thoroughly as possible:*

1) What does it take for you to feel successful?
2) What does it take for you to feel loved? by your kids, spouse, parents? by anyone else who is important to you?
3) What does it take for you to feel confident?
4) What does it take for you to feel you are excellent in any area of your life?

269

Every upset you've ever had with another human being has been a rules upset. You weren't upset with the person; you were upset that he or she violated one of your rules, one of your standards or beliefs about how things must or should be. In fact, you may have violated one of your own rules for how you should behave, think, or feel.

Next time you start getting upset with someone, remember that you're not upset with the person. You're reacting to *your* rules for the situation. Simply ask yourself, "What's more important in this case: my rules or my relationship with this person?"

Use this pattern interrupt to refocus on how to communicate in a more heartfelt fashion, and you'll find you can immediately transform a situation of conflict.

270

Don't expect people to abide by your rules if you don't clearly communicate what they are. And don't expect them to live by your rules if you're not willing to compromise and live by at least some of theirs.

Also remember that even if you've clarified all your rules in advance, misunderstandings can still occur. That's why **ongoing communication is so important.** Never assume when it comes to rules; *communicate.*

271

Some rules have more power to move us than others. Think of a rule you have in the area of health that you absolutely never violate. What words do you use to describe this "unbreakable" rule? Many would say, "I *must never* do drugs." By contrast, how do you phrase a rule you sometimes violate but regret later? Some would say, "Well, I *shouldn't* eat junk food..."

Having learned the rules of tens of thousands of people, I can tell you that **the rules you express as "I should not" you will break. The rules you express as "I must never" you will rarely if ever break.** I call the latter *threshold rules*.

How can you turn some of your "shoulds" into "musts" and immediately benefit from these behavioral changes?

272

Too many rules can make life unbearable. I once saw a television program that featured twenty families of quintuplets. Each set of parents was asked, "What is the most important thing you've learned for maintaining your sanity?" The one message echoed repeatedly was, **"Don't have too many rules."** Why? With that many bodies and personalities in motion, the law of averages dictates that, if you have too many rules, somebody's going to violate one of them just about any hour of the day —and you'll live in stress.

Wouldn't it be smarter simply to pick a few rules to live by, only the ones that are most important? I can tell you this: the fewer rules you have in your relationships, the happier you'll be.

273

By the way, I have a rule for you: while you're designing the new rules for your life, you must have fun! Get outrageous; explore the outer edges. Break your old rules. Create some crazy new ones. **You've been using rules all your life to limit yourself or to hold yourself back; why not get a few laughs at their expense?** Maybe in order to feel love, all you have to do is wiggle your little toe. It sounds weird, but who am I to decide what gives you pleasure?

THE KEYS TO AN EXPANDED LIFE

IDENTITY AND REFERENCES

●

*"If we all did the things we are capable of doing,
we would literally astound ourselves."*

—THOMAS A. EDISON

274

What makes you different from all the other people on this planet? One very important source of your uniqueness is your experiences. Everything you've ever done is recorded not only in your conscious memory, but also in your nervous system. **Everything you've ever seen, heard, touched, tasted, or smelled is tucked away in the giant file cabinet known as your brain.**

These conscious and unconscious memories are called *references*. These experiences are what we rely upon for certainty about what to believe, including some of our most important beliefs about who we are and what we're capable of.

275

What experiences have most powerfully shaped your life? Prior to attending one of my seminars, participants are asked to complete an in-depth questionnaire in which they list the five experiences they believe have most powerfully shaped their lives. **What's fascinating is that there are many people who've had the same experiences (references) but interpreted them in radically different ways.** Thus their lives are different today.

Two men lose their parents at a young age. One uses this experience as the reason to shut down emotionally from all intimate contact, while the other becomes one of the most outgoing and sensitive people you could possibly meet.

It's not only the references of our lives that shape us but, again, the meaning we attach to them.

276

You are the master designer of your life, whether you've realized it or not. **Think of all your experiences as a huge tapestry that can be laid out in whatever pattern you wish.** Each day you add a thread to the weaving...

Do you craft a curtain to hide behind, or do you fashion a magic carpet that will carry you to unequaled heights? Do you consciously rework the design so that the memories that empower you are the centerpiece of your masterwork?

277

Now take a moment to write down five of the experiences that have most powerfully shaped who you are.

Give not only a description of the event, but explain how it affected you. If you come up with anything that seems to have had negative consequences, immediately *reinterpret* it, no matter what it takes. **This may require some faith; it may call for a new perspective you never would have considered before.** Just remember that there is value in *all* human experience.

278

In order to accomplish anything, we need a sense of certainty. Our references help us to build this important emotional state. However, if we have no experience in (references for) doing something, how can we be certain about it? Realize you're not limited to your actual experience: **your imagination has unlimited references to support you.**

Remember that when Roger Bannister shattered the four-minute-mile record, it was due in large part to his having already accomplished the task in his mind's eye. His repeated visualizations of breaking the record provided him with the references, thus the conviction, to tap his ultimate physical potential.

How many barriers could you destroy if you merely used the force of your imagination to give you the reference experiences of breaking through?

279

Your imagination is ten times more potent than your willpower. **Unleashed, it provides a sense of certainty and tenacious vision that goes far beyond any limitations of the past.**

Andre Agassi recently told me that he'd won the Wimbledon tennis tournament *thousands* of times by the age of ten... *in his mind.* His consistent and vivid visualizations of victory provided him with the internal certainty that eventually brought him to this reality in the summer of 1992.

What dreams could you realize through the consistent employment of your imagination?

280

An easy way to immediately expand your personal "reference experience library" is by exploring the wealth of literature, stories, myths, poetry, and music available all around you. **Read books, watch movies and videotapes, attend plays, go to seminars, talk with strangers.** All references have power, and you never know which one could change your entire life.

281

The power of reading a great book is that you start thinking like the author. For those magical moments while you are immersed in the forests of Arden, you are William Shakespeare; while you are shipwrecked on Treasure Island, you are Robert Louis Stevenson; while you are communing with nature at Walden, you are Henry David Thoreau. You start to think as they think, feel as they feel, and use imagination as they would. **Their references become your own, and you carry these with you long after you've turned the last page.**

What fascinating, fun, enriching adventure can you take with a great book, entertaining play, or moving piece of music?

282

What if you adopted the belief that there are no bad experiences? Isn't it true that no matter what you go through in life—whether it's difficult or easy, painful or pleasurable—**every experience provides something of value** if you look for it?

Reflect on one of your "worst" experiences. The power to shape your life is gained by changing the meaning you link to an experience. Looking back, can you think of *any* ways in which it had a positive impact? Maybe you were fired, mugged, or involved in a car accident, but out of that experience you eventually gained a new resolve, or a new awareness or new sensitivity for others that caused you to grow as a person and measurably increased your ability to contribute.

283

Limited experiences create a limited life. If you desire enrichment and growth, you must increase your references by pursuing ideas and experiences that wouldn't be a part of your life if you didn't consciously seek them out. **Rarely will a great idea interrupt you; you must actively seek it out.**

What's something you've never even considered doing before that would open up whole new worlds to you?

284

Pursue some experiences you've never had before: Go scuba diving and explore the undersea world; see what life is like in a whole new environment... Spend an evening at the symphony, if it's not something you'd usually do, or hit a rock concert if that's what you habitually avoid ... Visit a children's hospital... Immerse yourself in a different culture, seeing the world through someone else's eyes... Take part in a ride-along program through your local police department.

Remember, any limitations you have in your life are probably just the result of limited reference experiences. Expand your references, and you'll immediately expand your life.

285

What are some new experiences you need to have? A good question to ask yourself is, "In order to achieve what I really want, what are some references I need?"

Consider what fun experiences you'd like to have. Think of some things to do that would be entertaining or just make you feel good.

Once you've brainstormed a list of new references to acquire, put a timeline on each. Decide when you're going to do every one of them. When will you learn to speak Spanish or Greek or Japanese? When are you going to take that hot-air-balloon ride? When are you going to visit a retirement home and sing carols? **When are you going to do something unusual and new?**

286

One of the most powerful references I share with my son is the experience we had one year while handing out baskets of food on Thanksgiving. I had encouraged my then four-year-old to deliver a basket to a man sleeping in the doorway of a public restroom. To my surprise, Jairek touched him on the shoulder and shouted, "Happy Thanksgiving!" All of a sudden, the man bolted upright and lunged for him. My heart leaped into my throat, and just as I started to spring forward, the man gently took Jairek's hand and kissed it. He whispered hoarsely, **"Thank you for caring . . ."** I wonder if there's a more powerful gift one could give to a child on Thanksgiving.

What moving experience could you share with someone you love?

287

You don't have to go on safari to expand your references; you can just go around the corner and help someone in your own community. Whole worlds open up with the addition of just one new reference. It could be one new thing you see or hear, a conversation or a movie or a seminar, something you read on the very next page—**you never know when it may happen.**

288

Get off the bench and step into the game of life! Let your imagination run wild with the possibilities of everything you could explore and experience—and begin immediately.

What new experience could you pursue today that would expand your life? What kind of person would you become as a result?

289

There's a force that shapes your life. It determines what you consider possible or impossible, what you attempt or pull back from, how you think and how you interact. **This force is the belief you have about who you are: your *identity*.**

We all have at least a subconscious way of defining ourselves, and this definition affects every part of our lives. If you see yourself as conservative, for example, you will move and even talk differently than if you considered yourself to be outrageous. A change in your personal definition will instantly change the talents you express, the behaviors you demonstrate, and the aspirations you pursue. It's the filter through which every decision is made, the core belief through which you interpret all of life's experience.

290

Have you ever said, "I can't do that! I'm just not like that!"? If you've ever used this phrase, you've hit the boundary of how you've defined yourself in the past, and it's affecting the quality of your present-day life. Ask yourself, "Where did these beliefs about who I am come from, and how old are they?" **Maybe it's time to update your identity.** Did you choose it consciously, or is it the sum total of what other people have told you, significant events in your life, and other factors that occurred without your awareness or approval?

If you were to begin to define yourself differently, in a way that's more empowering and accurate for who you are today, how would you describe who you've become?

291

All of us need to expand our view of who we are and what we're capable of. We need to make certain that the labels we put on ourselves are not limits but enhancements, that we add to all that's already good within us. **Be aware: whatever you consistently attach to the words "I am" you will become.** For example, some people say, "I'm a lazy person." They may not be lazy; they just have uninspiring goals.

Are you defining yourself in ways that create limits? Are these limits becoming a self-fulfilling prophecy? If so, change them now!

292

Any time we make a change in our lives, others in our environment will either be a help or a hindrance to our making permanent progress. If they continue to think of us in the same way as they have in the past, then their sense of certainty (beliefs) about who we've been can actually serve as a negative anchor, temporarily pulling us back into the old limiting emotions and beliefs that were once a part of our identity.

We must be aware that **we hold the ultimate power to define who we are.** Our past does not determine our present or future. *Take action and claim your new, empowering identity, starting today.*

293

If you've tried repeatedly to make a positive change yet continually fallen short, chances are that you were attempting to switch to a behavior that was inconsistent with your beliefs about who you are. **In order to produce the most profound and rapid improvements in the quality of your life, you must shift, change, or expand your *identity*.**

For example, rather than merely try to stop a behavior like drinking, you could expand your identity to that of a vitally healthy person dedicated to peak performance. As a natural consequence of this decision, abusing alcohol is something you'd never even consider.

What is an identity crisis? Perhaps the best definition for this relatively common experience is that it occurs when people act inconsistently with who they believe they are, which causes them to question everything in their lives. But do any of us really know who we are completely? I suspect not.

Having an identity that is specifically linked to one's age or appearance would definitely set someone up for pain, a future crisis; after all, these things are bound to change. But if we have a broader sense of who we are, maybe even a spiritual definition, our identities can never be threatened.

Certainly we're more than our physical bodies. So what makes you unique?

295

Take a moment now to identify who you are. Decide to be curious and playful about answering the question, **"Who are you?"**

Do you define yourself by your past, present, or future accomplishments? by your profession? by your income? by your life roles? by your spiritual beliefs? by your physical attributes? or by something that transcends all of these categories?

296

***If you were to look up your name in the dictionary,* how would you be defined?** Would three words just about cover it, or would your epic narrative consume page after page—or even demand a volume of its own?

Right now, write down the definition you might find in Webster's under your name.

297

If you were to create an I.D. card **that would represent who you *truly* are, what would be on it—and what would you leave off?** Would you include a photograph or physical description, or do you consider those unimportant? Would the card list your vital statistics? accomplishments? values? emotions? beliefs? aspirations? motto?

Take a minute to design your I.D. card, a very personal piece of identification you could use to show someone who you really are.

298

If some aspects of your identity create pain for you, why hang on to them? They're simply what you've decided to identify with *up until now.*

Take a cue from the wondrous imagination that fills the heart and soul of any child. One day he's Zorro, the righter of wrongs. The next he's Hercules, the strongest man on earth. And today he's Grandpa, his own real-life hero. Identity shifts can be among the most joyous, magical, and liberating experiences of life. In a moment, we can completely redefine ourselves, or we can simply decide to let our real selves shine through, uncovering a giant identity that is more than our behaviors, more than our past, more than any label we've been giving ourselves.

299

If you could be anyone you wanted, what would your identity consist of? *Make a list today of all the elements you'd want to include.* Who already has these characteristics you aspire to having? Can these people serve as role models? Imagine yourself fusing with this new identity. Picture how you'd breathe. How would you walk? How would you talk? How would you think? How would you feel?

Rejoice in the power you have right now to change any part of your identity simply by *deciding to*.

300

If you genuinely want to expand your identity—and your life—then consciously decide who you want to be. **Get excited, be like a kid again, and describe in detail who you've decided you are today.**

Take some time now to jot down an expanded list—and don't limit yourself.

301

The people we spend time with have a powerful influence on our perceptions of who we are. **As you develop a plan of action to back up your new identity, pay special attention to the people you surround yourself with.**

Will your friends, family, and business associates reinforce or tear down the identity you're creating?

302

Commit to your new identity by broadcasting it to everyone around you. **The most important broadcast, however, is to yourself.** Use your new label to describe yourself every single day, and it will become conditioned within you.

303

This very moment you can start living the new identity you've chosen. Ask yourself, "What more *can* I be? What more *will* I be? Who am I becoming *now?*"

Commit to yourself that, regardless of the environment, you will consistently act as a person who is already achieving the goals you've set. Breathe as this person. Move as this person. Respond to other people as this person. Treat people with the kind of dignity, respect, compassion, and love that this person would.

If you decide to think, feel, and act as the kind of person you want to be, you will become that person.

304

You are now at a crossroads. **Forget your past. Who are you *now*?**
Don't think about who you have been. Who have you decided to become?
  Make this decision consciously. Make it carefully. Make it powerfully.
Then act upon it!

PUTTING IT ALL TOGETHER

HEALTH, FINANCES, RELATIONSHIPS, AND CODE OF CONDUCT

●

"Go put your creed into your deed."

—RALPH WALDO EMERSON

305

Start reaping the rewards **of some of the strategies, tools, and daily lessons in self-mastery that you've been learning.** As you read each page in this section, you'll focus on several major areas—physical, financial, and relationships—and create a method for ensuring that you live in accordance with your highest standards each and every day.

306

Just as you've learned to condition your nervous system to produce the behaviors that will give you the results you want, **your physical destiny depends on how you condition your metabolism and muscles** to produce the levels of energy and fitness you desire.

What do you do regularly to take care of your body and produce the level of health you desire?

307

What causes the human body to function at peak efficiency? The incredible accomplishment of Stu Mittleman illustrates the power of some basic principles. **Mittleman broke the world's long-distance record by running over 1,000 miles in 11 days, 19 hours—averaging 84 miles per day!** Perhaps even more amazing is that, according to witnesses, he looked *better* at the end of his run than at the starting line. He suffered no injuries—not even a blister.

What allowed him to stretch his body to its limits and still maximize his potential without injuring it? First, by devoting years of training to his mind and body, Mittleman proved that we can adapt to anything if we make the right demands upon ourselves *incrementally*.

308

What was the second distinction that enabled Stu Mittleman to set a new record in long-distance running? Simply that **health and fitness are not the same.**

What is *fitness?* According to Dr. Philip Maffetone, it's "the physical ability to perform athletic activity." *Health*, however, is defined much more broadly as "the state where all the systems of the body...are working in an optimal way." Many people think that fitness implies health, but the two don't necessarily go hand in hand. If you achieve fitness at the expense of health, you may not live long enough to enjoy your spectacular physique.

For you, which comes first? Have you created a balance between health and fitness?

309

So how do we maximize our health? **The best way is to understand the difference between aerobic and anaerobic exercise, between endurance and power.** *Aerobic* means "with oxygen" and refers to moderate exercise sustained over a period of time. If you activate your endurance with aerobic exercise, you burn *fat* as your primary fuel. *Anaerobic,* on the other hand, means "without oxygen" and refers to exercise that produces short bursts of power. Anaerobic exercise burns *glycogen* as its primary fuel and causes the body to store fat.

Do you consider yourself healthy? fit? neither?

310

Why do so many Americans experience fatigue? **Out of the desire to produce the greatest results in the shortest period of time, many people lead anaerobic lifestyles inundated with stress and demands, compounded by the way they exercise.** By exercising anaerobically, they deplete their systems of glycogen. Their metabolism then turns to blood sugar as a secondary source of fuel, causing headaches, fatigue, and other problems.

How can you shift from anaerobic to aerobic exercise? *Simply by slowing down.* According to Dr. Philip Maffetone, most types of exercise, such as walking, jogging, biking, and swimming, can be either aerobic or anaerobic. Lower heart rates make them aerobic, while higher heart rates make them anaerobic.

Do you need to slow down? in your exercise? in your lifestyle?

311

To turn your body into a fat-burning machine, you must train your metabolism to operate consistently in aerobic fashion. **Dr. Maffetone suggests a period of two to eight months of exclusively aerobic exercise.** To achieve a balance between health and fitness, anaerobic workouts can then be incorporated into your routine one to three times a week.

Whom do you need to consult to optimize your health? What resources could you call upon?

312

The British philosopher Ludwig Wittgenstein wrote, **"The human body is the best picture of the human soul."**
What does your body say about your inner self?

313

The most important element in producing health is probably oxygen. Without it, cells become weakened and die.

To avoid depleting your body of oxygen during exercise, you need to know whether you've moved beyond aerobic into anaerobic activity.

Answer the following questions:

1) Can you talk while exercising (aerobic), or are you too winded (anaerobic)?

2) Is your breathing steady and audible (aerobic), or more labored (anaerobic)?

3) Does the exercise feel pleasurable though tiring (aerobic), or do you definitely feel pushed (anaerobic)?

4) On a scale from 0 to 10, with 0 representing minimum exertion and 10 being the most intense, what's your score? Ideally your evaluation would be between 6 and 7; if you've exceeded 7 then you've moved into the anaerobic range.

314

Here's how to begin incorporating consistent, pleasurable exercise into your lifestyle:

1) Determine whether your regular exercise is aerobic or anaerobic: Do you wake up feeling tired? Do you feel famished, experience wild mood swings, and/or feel aches and pains after working out? Does that same layer of fat cling to you despite your most diligent efforts? If you answered yes to some or all of these questions, chances are that you're exercising anaerobically.

2) Purchase a portable heart-rate monitor to help you stay within your optimum aerobic training zone. It's one of the best investments you'll ever make.

3) Develop a plan to begin conditioning your metabolism to burn fat and produce consistent levels of energy. Stick to this plan for at least ten days.

315

Few things in life are more important to master than your relationships. Success is unfulfilling unless you have someone to share it with—indeed, the most highly sought emotion is that of connection. In the next few days let's consider six organizing principles that are fundamental to the success of any relationship, especially your love relationships.

First, you must know the values and rules of the person with whom you are involved. No matter how much you love someone, no matter how intimate your connection, there will be upsets and debilitating stresses if you are constantly breaking each other's rules.

If you don't know (or have forgotten) your partner's rules, find them out. If it's been a while since you've discussed them, it's a good idea to check in again.

316

The only way a relationship will last is if you **see it as a place you go to *give*,** not a place that you go to take.
   In your relationship, what is the most valuable thing you give?

317

To nurture a relationship, **be aware of any warning signals that may surface.** By identifying them and intervening immediately, you can eliminate them before they get out of hand.

Are there any early warning signs in your relationships that you need to heed? What are some actions you can take today to "kill the monster while it's little," before it has a chance to grow out of proportion?

318

So many times, relationships break up without people even knowing what went wrong. **The most important way to ensure success in any relationship is to *communicate clearly* up front.** Make sure your rules are known and met.

Develop pattern interrupts with your partner to prevent the kinds of arguments where you can't even remember what the disagreement is about anymore, only that you've got to win.

Use Transformational Vocabulary to keep upsets from being blown out of proportion. For example, instead of saying, "I can't stand it when you do that," say, "I'd prefer it if you did this instead."

319

Is your love relationship one of the highest priorities in your life? If not, it will take a back seat to all the other, more urgent things that happen every day, and your passion will gradually dissipate.

Don't allow familiarity to habituate you to the intense excitement and gratitude you feel for having someone special in your life.

320

If you want your relationship to last, never threaten it. Just making the statement, "If you do that, then I'm leaving," creates the possibility. **Instead, focus each day on making the relationship better.** Every couple I've known who's had a lasting and fulfilling relationship has made it a rule, no matter how angry or hurt they've ever felt, always to hold on to the unquestioned existence of the relationship.

321

One of the best things you can do each day is to experience anew what you love about the person you're in a relationship with. Reinforce your feelings of connection and renew your feelings of intimacy and attraction by constantly asking, **"How did I get so lucky to have you in my life?"** Embark on a never-ending quest to find new ways to surprise and show your appreciation for each other. Don't take your lover for granted —find and create those special moments that can make your relationship legendary!

What is something you can do today for someone you love?

322

Are you committed to having the love relationship of your dreams? Here are some Cardinal Rules of Relationships:

1) Spend time with your significant other and find out what's most important to each of you. What are your highest values in the relationship, and what must happen for each of you to feel that those values are being fulfilled?

2) Decide that it's more important for you to be in love than to be right. If you ever start insisting that you have to be right, break your own pattern. If necessary, stop the conflict until you can return to it in a more resourceful state for finding a resolution.

323

MORE CARDINAL RULES OF RELATIONSHIPS

3) Create pattern interrupts you both agree to use when things become most heated. Use the most bizarre or humorous pattern interrupts you can devise; make them a private, personal joke between the two of you.

4) When you feel resistance, communicate it with softeners such as, "I know it's only my own idiosyncrasy, but when you do that, it makes me feel just the slightest smidge cranky."

5) Plan regular date nights together, preferably once a week, or twice a month at the minimum. Dream up fun, romantic things to do.

6) Make sure you get a good, 60-second wet kiss every day!

324

Many people make the mistake of thinking that all the problems in their lives would disappear if they just had enough money. Yet earning more money, in and of itself, rarely frees people. **It's equally ridiculous, however, to tell yourself that greater financial freedom and mastery of your finances wouldn't offer you more opportunities to grow, share, and create value for yourself and others.**

325

Creating wealth is simple. Yet most people never do so because they have holes—value and belief conflicts—in their financial foundations. **The most common reason financial success eludes people is that they have mixed feelings about money.** While they may value what they believe it would provide, they may also believe they'd have to work too hard for it, or that it would corrupt them, or that anyone who is rich must have taken advantage of others.

Another common reason why many people never master money is that they think it's too complex and should be left to the "experts." While it always makes sense to get great coaching, we all must be trained to take responsibility for and understand the consequences of our financial decisions.

326

After years of studying the most successful people in our culture, I've discovered five keys to financial mastery. **The first key is the ability to *create* wealth.** If you can find a way to increase the value of what you do by at least ten to fifteen times, then you can easily increase your income.

Start by asking yourself, "How can I be worth more to this company? How can I help it to achieve more in less time? In what ways could I help cut costs while increasing profitability and quality? What new systems could I implement? What new technology could I use that would give this company a competitive edge?"

327

The second key to financial mastery is to *maintain* your wealth. **The only way to do this is to spend less than you earn, and invest the difference.**

328

Saving money is a worthwhile goal, but by itself it won't bring you economic abundance. **The third key to mastering your finances is to *increase* your wealth.** To accomplish this, you must spend less than you earn, invest the difference, and *reinvest your returns for compounded growth.* Compounding puts your money to work for you by increasing it exponentially. The pace at which you achieve financial independence is in direct proportion to your willingness to reinvest—not spend—the profits of your past investments.

329

No one wants to be a "target." **The fourth key to financial mastery is to *protect* your wealth.** In today's litigious atmosphere, many people who are wealthy actually feel more insecure than when they had fewer assets, simply because they know that now they could be sued at any moment, sometimes for completely frivolous reasons. The good news is that there are legal avenues for protecting your assets, as long as you're not currently involved in a lawsuit.

Do you need to consider asset protection? Even if you aren't yet concerned with this issue, now is the time to start consulting the experts and modeling the masters, just as you would in any other important area of your life.

330

Don't wait too long to start taking pleasure in economic abundance. **The fifth key to financial mastery is to *enjoy* your wealth.** Most people wait until they've accumulated a certain amount of money to start enjoying themselves. But unless you link pleasure to creating value and earning money, you'll never keep it long term. So reward yourself occasionally with jackpots (surprise bonuses).

Also consider tithing. By giving away a portion of what you earn, you teach yourself that you have more than enough. True wealth is an emotion: *a sense of absolute abundance.* Money has no value unless we share its positive impact with the people we care about, and as we discover ways to contribute in proportion to our incomes, we tap into one of life's greatest joys.

331

Begin now to take control of your financial future.

1) Brainstorm all your beliefs about money. Question your limiting beliefs, and strengthen the empowering ones. Use the six steps of NAC to condition your new patterns.

2) Figure out how to add more value to your business or employer, whether you're paid for it or not. Decide to add at least ten times more value than you currently do.

3) Commit to deducting at least 10 percent from your paycheck and investing it in your portfolio.

4) Obtain good coaching to help you make intelligent investment decisions.

5) Create a small jackpot to start associating pleasure to financial success. For whom could you do something special? How could you reinforce yourself for getting started today?

332

It's great to have a hierarchy of values to which you are committed. But without measuring, how do you know whether you're truly living them on a day-to-day or moment-to-moment basis? Contribution may be one of your top values, but how consistently do you do it? Love may be high on your list, but can you think of lots of times when you haven't been loving?

The solution is simple: **Create your own personal Code of Conduct.** How? Keep reading . . .

333

Can you remember the last time you felt absolutely clear about how to act in any situation, no matter what crazy thing might come up? Most of us never feel this kind of certainty unless we decide in advance upon a set of characteristics we're committed to adopting and living every day of our lives. Actually writing these down, creating a personal "Code of Conduct," provides a superlative road map for all of life's travels.

1) Make a list of all the states you are committed to being every day in order to live according to your highest principles and values. Make the list long enough to ensure you experience the richness and variety you deserve, yet short enough that you can truly achieve these states every day.

334

YOUR CODE OF CONDUCT (Continued)

2) Next to each characteristic, write your rule for how you will know you are feeling it. For example: "I am being cheerful when I smile at people" or "I am being grateful when I remember all the good things I have in my life."

3) Commit to experience each of these states at least once a day. You might want to write your Code of Conduct on a piece of paper you carry with you everywhere, or have copies of it on your desk at work or by your bed. Periodically review your list and ask, "Which of these states have I already experienced today? Which of them have I not—and how will I accomplish it by the end of the day?"

THE ULTIMATE GIFT

CONTRIBUTION

•

*"Someday, after we have mastered the winds,
the waves, the tide and gravity, we shall harness
for God the energies of love. Then, for the second
time in the history of the world, man will have
discovered fire."*

—TEILHARD DE CHARDIN

335

For more than a decade, I've had the unique honor of working with people from virtually all walks of life, from the privileged to the impoverished. One thing stands clear: Regardless of stature, **only those who have learned the power of sincere and selfless contribution experience life's deepest joy—true fulfillment.**

336

We've all had close encounters with a feeling of selfless contribution: providing a friend with a helping hand, showing a child how to master a problem, assisting a co-worker with a difficult project, helping an elderly person down a treacherous flight of stairs. **These experiences give us a moment of exultation in which we catch a glimmer of our essential selves.** And it moves us to be truly awe-inspired by those who *consistently* give of themselves.

This section is your invitation to become a consistent giver, to join a spirited team that is committed to sharing the gift of possibility with those who seek to improve the quality of their lives.

337

The conscience of an entire nation received a wake-up call through the simple yet courageous actions of one man. When Sam LaBudde signed onboard the *Maria Luisa* as a temporary crew member, he risked his life to videotape the carnage wrought upon dolphins by tuna fishing.

By 1991—just four years later—the world's largest tuna canner, Starkist, announced it would no longer pack tuna caught in purse seine nets. Other canners followed suit just hours later. While the fight is not yet over, this man's contribution to the effort saved countless dolphin lives and undoubtedly helped to restore some measure of balance to an incredibly delicate ecosystem.

What could you do with a little creativity and courage that could make a difference for others—and even the world?

338

Wouldn't it take a superhuman effort to solve the world's problems? Nothing could be further from the truth. **Whatever results we're experiencing in our lives are the accumulation of a host of small decisions we've made as individuals, a family, a community, a society, and a species.**

Large solutions start with individuals who take small but consistent actions that build into worldwide change.

339

Every single one of the national and global problems facing us today was set in motion by human behavior. The good news is that, since our behavior is the root cause, we have the power to change it! There are actions every one of us can take in our own homes, businesses, and communities that will initiate a chain of specific, positive consequences. **The only limit to our impact is our imagination and commitment.**

340

How does a person make a difference? **The history of the world is simply a chronicle of the deeds of a small number of ordinary people who had extraordinary levels of commitment.** Those individuals who had the power to make a meaningful difference in the quality of our lives are the men and women we call *heroes.*

Who are your heroes?

341

I believe that you and I—and everyone we'll ever meet—have the innate capacity to be heroic, to take daring, courageous, and noble steps to make life better for others, even when in the short term it seems to be at our own expense.

The capacity to do the right thing, to dare to take a stand and make a difference, is within you now. The question is: When the moment arrives, will you remember you're a hero and selflessly respond in support of those in need?

342

Surmounting difficulty is the crucible that forms character.

343

You might assume that Mother Teresa was born to heroism. But as a teaching nun in a relatively wealthy section of Calcutta, she rarely crossed the poorer parts of town. One evening, however, she heard the cries of a dying woman. Mother rushed to her aid and spent the rest of the night unsuccessfully seeking aid at various hospitals. When the woman finally died in her arms, Mother's life was transformed. In one defining moment, perhaps the divine moment, she vowed that as long as she lived no one within her reach would ever die without dignity and love.

Is there a specific time in your life you can point to as a defining moment?

344

What makes a hero? **A hero is a person who courageously contributes under even the most trying circumstances;** a hero is an individual who acts unselfishly and who demands more from himself or herself than others would expect; a hero is someone who defies adversity by doing what he or she believes is right in spite of fear.

345

A hero is not someone who is "perfect." We'd have no heroes if this were our standard. We all make mistakes, but that doesn't invalidate the contributions we make in the course of our lives. **Perfection is not heroism; humanity is.**

346

How can we tackle giant social issues? Know that within each of us glimmers the light of heroism, just waiting to be fanned into a mighty flame. **The first key is to hold ourselves to a higher standard and fulfill this promise.**

347

When society's problems seem overwhelming, each of us can take immediate control by changing our beliefs. **Most important, we must *stop* believing that the challenges facing us are permanent and pervasive, that one person's actions don't matter.** Did Gandhi give up because he was only one man? Did Mother Teresa surrender her passion because she was just one nun fighting the pain of the impoverished? Did Ed Roberts buckle under the strain of being a lone advocate for the rights of disabled people?

Do something today to demonstrate that your actions make a difference. Volunteer to comfort crack babies at your local hospital... Serve dinner to homeless people... Help an adult learn to read... Teach parenting skills to teenage mothers... Take a bouquet of balloons to a retirement home.

348

What would happen if you cultivated a friendship with a homeless person and offered some experiences that he or she may not have enjoyed in a long time, perhaps ever? How would a trip to the movie theater or beauty parlor make someone living on the streets feel? Special? cared for? worthy? Remember that new references provide the fabric for new beliefs and identities. **Remember, too, that small efforts can add up to giant results.**

Do something this week: Decide now what you'll do, schedule it, and make it happen! I promise you that the rewards of giving far outweigh any efforts you may make.

349

Our everyday decisions will shape the world we pass on to future generations. **What do you put on your dinner plate? What cosmetics do you use? What household products do you buy?** These lifestyle choices determine in a small yet undeniable way such things as how much carbon dioxide is released into our atmosphere and how many plant and animal species will be eliminated each day.

By the same token, the decisions you make every day can help stop the destruction of the rain forests, restore the delicate balance of our ecosystem, and create a legacy of hope for generations to come.

350

How can we make a difference in the future of our children? **First, we can take an active role in determining the quality of their education.**

Could your children's teachers benefit by understanding what you've learned in this book? Consider the power of questions, global metaphors, Transformational Vocabulary, values, rules, and Neuro-Associative Conditioning. By sharing what you know, you can truly have an impact.

351

Few things could be more dangerous than letting your children fall into the trap of thinking that what they do doesn't matter. **Teach them the consequences of their actions.** Show them that even small decisions and actions, consistently made, have far-reaching effects.

How can you be an inspiring role model today? How can you show them the power of dedication, of integrity, of commitment? How can you demonstrate what's possible?

352

We don't need to wait until we have a grandiose master plan to make a difference. We can have impact in a moment, in doing the smallest things, in making what often seem like insignificant decisions. It's true that most of our heroes are hidden behind what appear to be small acts done consistently. Look around you. **There are heroes everywhere.**

353

How would you feel if someone had a heart attack in your presence, but you were CPR-certified and knew what to do? What if your concerted efforts actually resulted in saving a life?

The feeling of contribution you would get from that experience would give you a greater sense of fulfillment and joy than anything you've ever felt in your life—greater than any acknowledgment anyone could possibly give you, greater than any amount of money you could possibly earn, greater than any achievement you could possibly have.

Sign up today for a CPR class so that if and when an emergency arises and someone needs your help, you can deliver!

354

Something as simple as a smile can make a person's day. What if you were in a grocery store and, instead of wandering aimlessly from the artichokes to the zucchini, you actually noticed and *acknowledged* each person with a cheerful grin as you passed? **What if you gave sincere compliments to strangers?** Could you, in that moment, change their emotional state enough so that the smile or compliment could be passed on to the next person they saw as well? Could there be a domino effect set in motion by that one action?

How would doing all this affect your mental/emotional state— your very identity?

355

On your way home from work, what if you decided to stop at a retirement center and strike up a conversation with someone there? How would it make them feel if you were to ask, **"What are some of the most important lessons you've learned in your life?"** I'll bet they'd have plenty to tell you!

What if you stopped at your community hospital, visited a patient, and helped brighten the afternoon? What do you think it would mean to a lonely soul to have a stranger care about him or her? How would it make this person feel?

Just as important, how will it make you feel—about yourself, and this gift called life?

356

Why are so many people afraid to make even the smallest effort to help others? One of the most common reasons is that they are just embarrassed. They're afraid of being rejected or appearing foolish. But you know what? **If you want to play the game of life and win, you've got to play full out.** You've got to be willing to feel stupid, and you've got to be willing to try things that might not work. Otherwise, how can you innovate, how can you grow, how can you discover who you really are?

357

In the deepest part of ourselves, we all want to do what we believe is right, to go beyond ourselves, to commit our energy, time, emotion, and capital to a larger cause. **We respond not just to our psychological needs, but to our moral imperative to do more and be more than anyone could expect.** Nothing gives us a greater sense of personal satisfaction than contribution.

In what ways do you give unselfishly?

358

Do you realize that if everyone in the country (except the very young or elderly) were to volunteer just three hours a week, **our nation would reap the rewards of over 320 million hours of much-needed manpower** dedicated to the causes we care most about? And if each of us were to contribute five hours, the figure would jump to half a billion hours with a monetary equivalent in the trillions?

What social or political or medical problems do you think we could conquer with this kind of commitment?

359

Don't look for heroes. Be one!

360

Life is a balance **between giving and receiving,** between taking care of yourself and taking care of others.

The next time you see someone in trouble, instead of just passing by or feeling guilty about being unable to help, get excited about what you can do. Perhaps you can offer something as simple as a kind word or a smile that will cause this person to think about himself or herself in a new way. Maybe you can help this person begin to feel appreciated and loved.

361

Live fully while you're here. Experience everything. Take care of yourself and your friends. Have fun, be crazy, be weird. Go out and screw up! You're going to anyway, so you may as well enjoy the process! Take the opportunity to learn from your mistakes: Find the cause of your problem and eliminate it. **Don't try to be perfect; just be an excellent example of being human.**

362

One of the greatest gifts we've received from our Creator is the gift of anticipation and suspense. **How boring life would be if we knew in advance how it would all turn out!** In the next few moments, something could happen that could change the entire direction and quality of your life in an instant. We must learn to love change, for it is the only thing that is certain.

363

What can change your life? Many things: a moment of deep thought and a few decisions as you complete this book could change everything. So could a conversation with a friend; a tape; a seminar; a movie; or a big, fat, juicy "problem" that causes you to expand and become more. This is the awakening you seek. **So live in an attitude of positive expectancy, knowing that everything that happens in your life benefits you in some way.** Know that you are guided along a path of never-ending growth and learning, and with it, the path of everlasting love.

364

Remember to expect miracles ... because you are one.

365

Be a bearer of the light and a force for good. Share your gifts; share your passion. And may God bless you.

I look forward to meeting you personally one day soon!

With love and respect,

Anthony Robbins

ABOUT THE ANTHONY ROBBINS COMPANIES

As an alliance of several organizations sharing the same mission, the Anthony Robbins Companies (ARC) are dedicated to constantly improve the quality of life for individuals and organizations who truly desire it. Offering cutting-edge technologies for the management of human emotion and behavior, ARC empowers individuals to recognize and *utilize* their unlimited choices.

Listed below are just some of the useful resources ARC offers you or your organization. For more information and a complete list of available services and products, please call **1-800-445-8183.**

Robbins Research International, Inc.
This research and marketing arm of Anthony Robbins' consulting and personal development businesses conducts public and corporate seminars worldwide. Topics range from peak performance and financial mastery to negotiating and corporate reengineering.

Anthony Robbins Foundation™

A non-profit organization committed to consistently reaching and assisting individuals often forgotten by society—homeless people, the elderly, children, and the prison population—the Anthony Robbins Foundation and its volunteers provide the finest resources for inspiration, education, training, and development.

Personal Power: 30 Days to Success™

The *Personal Power* program is a set of 24 tapes that takes you through a 30-day step-by-step process for producing specific changes mentally, emotionally, physically, and financially. The techniques and strategies are immediately applicable, and each day's action builds momentum toward a greater quality of life.

Anthony Robbins' PowerTalk!™

Each month, Anthony Robbins interviews one of the most successful men and women of our time (e.g., Norman Cousins, Sir John Templeton, Ken Blanchard). In these interviews he extracts the fundamental strategies of their achievements, whether in the areas of leadership, physical vitality and health, or financial success. With each edition of *PowerTalk!* you also receive a second audiotape in which Anthony Robbins shares his newest strategies for improving your personal and professional life. Also included is a 20-plus-page summary of a national best-selling book so that you can keep yourself up to date on the newest strategies available in the marketplace today.

Robbins Research International, Inc.
9191 Towne Centre Drive
Suite 600
San Diego, CA 92122
1-800-445-8183

TREE EVENT MANAGEMENT
If you want to see **Tony Robbins** LIVE at one of his
"Unleash the Power Within" seminars in Europe.
Simply call or fax us today and we will forward to you
a complimentary brochure and a FREE audio tape
featuring **Tony Robbins** LIVE.

Telephone +44 (0) 207 351 9100

Fax +44 (0) 207 376 7476

Take action NOW